STUDY MANUAL

TO ACCOMPANY
VANDER-SHERMAN-LUCIANO

STUDY MANUAL

TO ACCOMPANY
VANDER-SHERMAN-LUCIANO

HUMAN PHYSIOLOGY

**SIXTH
EDITION**

DONNA M. VAN WYNSBERGHE
University of Wisconsin-Milwaukee

McGRAW-HILL, INC.

New York   St. Louis   San Francisco   Auckland   Bogotá
Caracas   Hamburg   Lisbon   London   Madrid   Mexico City
Milan   Montreal   New Delhi   San Juan   São Paulo
Singapore   Sydney   Tokyo   Toronto

This book is printed on recycled paper containing 10% post consumer waste.

STUDY MANUAL to Accompany Vander/Sherman/Luciano: HUMAN PHYSIOLOGY

3 4 5 6 7 8 9 MAL MAL 9 0 9 8 7 6 5 4

ISBN 0-07-066993-7

This book was set in Bembo by Pat McCarney.
The editor was Pamela Wirt;
the production supervisor was Paula Keller.

CONTENTS

CONTENTS

INTRODUCTION

This study manual is written to closely complement the textbook *Human Physiology,* 6th ed., by Vander, Sherman, and Luciano. A study manual is intended to be a guide to studying the content of the material covered, and this one is so intended. The questions are of a mixed variety and difficulty. The answers are at the end of each chapter for easy reference. I highly recommend that you, as a student of physiology, work through these questions diligently; diagram, draw, label, and fill in the blanks when asked; write notes in the margins; take time to think; and share your learning with others. You will find that if you can draw, diagram, write, or say it, you know it. Try it. And most importantly, I hope you will enjoy the learning of these physiological principles in your study of physiology.

I would like to thank David E. Cochrane, Tufts University, and Jerome B. Senturia, Cleveland State University, for providing feedback on preliminary chapters. I am also extremely grateful for the gentle, gracious guidance of Pamela Wirt of McGraw-Hill, Inc., in the preparation of this study guide as well as her detailed "line-by-line" review of every sentence and figure in creating the final version of the manuscript. Thank you, Pam.

D. M. Van Wynsberghe, Ph.D.

CHAPTER

I

A FRAMEWORK
FOR HUMAN PHYSIOLOGY

MECHANISM AND CAUSALITY

1. How does a "mechanist" view life?

2. How does a "vitalist" view life?

3. Define and give an example of teleology.

A SOCIETY OF CELLS

Cells: The Basic Units

4. List several functions that all cells perform.

5. Match:

   a. organs

   b. tissues

   c. cells

   d. cell differentiation

   a. ___ simple structural units that can divide and carry on life

   b. ___ the process of transforming an unspecialized cell into a specialized cell

   c. ___ an aggregate of a single type of specialized cells

   d. ___ several tissue types joined together

6. List the levels of cellular organization from a single cell up to a total organism (human being).

7. Four functional categories of cells are:

   a.

   b.

   c.

   d.

8. Give a brief description of the function of each of the above specialized cells.

   a.

   b.

   c.

   d.

Tissues

9. Four general tissue types are:

   a.

   b.

   c.

   d.

Organs and Organ Systems

10. List the 10 organ systems of the body and give an example of an organ in each of the organ systems.

    a.

    b.

    c.

    d.

    e.

    f.

    g.

    h.

    i.

    j.

THE INTERNAL ENVIRONMENT AND HOMEOSTASIS

11. The internal environment surrounding each cell is known as _____ fluid.

12. The concept of maintaining the internal environment relatively constant is known as _____ .

BODY-FLUID COMPARTMENTS

13. Extracellular fluid can be divided into _____ and _____ .

14. Eighty percent of the extracellular fluid is (*interstitial, plasma*).

15. The chemical compositions of the interstitial fluid and plasma are similar except that plasma has a higher _____ concentration.

16. Intracellular and extracellular fluid have similar chemical compositions. (*true, false*)

17. Describe or diagram how the 42 L of total body water is compartmentalized.

Review the SUMMARY and REVIEW QUESTIONS at the end of this chapter in your textbook.

CHAPTER 1 ANSWER KEY

1. All phenomena of life are described in terms of physical and chemical laws.

2. Some "vital force" beyond physical and chemical laws is required to explain or describe phenomena of life.

3. Teleology is an explanation of events in terms of purpose. Examples include: it is raining because the sun is not out; there is blood pressure because the heart is beating.

4. Exchange materials with their immediate environment, obtain energy from organic nutrients, synthesize complex molecules, undergo cell duplication.

5. a. c   b. d   c. b   d. a

6. Cells differentiate into specialized cells which become tissues which form functional units known as organs which form organ systems which become a whole functional being.

7. a. muscle cells   c. epithelial cells
   b. nerve cells   d. connective tissue cells

8. a. Muscle cells produce force and movement.
   b. Nerve cells initiate and conduct electric signals.
   c. Epithelial cells selectively secrete and transport ions and organic molecules.
   d. Connective tissue cells connect, support, and anchor structures of the body.

9. a. muscle   c. epithelial
   b. nerve   d. connective

10. a. circulation (heart)   f. immune (lymph nodes)
    b. respiration (lungs)   g. nervous (brain)
    c. digestion (stomach)   h. endocrine (pancreas)
    d. urinary (kidneys)   i. reproductive (ovaries)
    e. musculoskeletal (muscle)   j. integumentary (skin)

11. extracellular

12. homeostasis

13. interstitial (intercellular), plasma

14. interstitial

15. protein

16. false

17. intracellular water: 28 L; extracellular water: 14 L [consisting of 11 L interstitial water (80 percent) and 3 L plasma (20 percent)] (See Fig. 1.3, p. 7)

CHAPTER
2
CHEMICAL COMPOSITION OF THE BODY

ATOMS

1. The units of matter that form all chemical substances are called _____ .

2. Three subatomic particles in atoms are:

   a.

   b.

   c.

3. The atomic particles located in the nucleus are:

   a.

   b.

4. The electric charges on each of the particles in an atom are:

5. Most of the mass of an atom is located in the _____ .

Atomic Number

6. The atomic number of an atom is determined by:

Atomic Weight

7. The atomic weight of an atom is approximately equal to its number of _____ plus its number of _____ .

8. One gram atomic mass of a chemical element is:

Atomic Composition of the Body

9. The four major elements that constitute over 99 percent of the atoms of the body are:

10. The seven essential mineral elements in the body are:

MOLECULES

11. A molecule is defined as:

12. The molecular formula for water is _____ and for glucose is _____ .

Covalent Chemical Bonds

13. Describe a covalent bond.

14. The number of covalent bonds formed by the following are:
    a. Hydrogen:
    b. Oxygen:
    c. Nitrogen:
    d. Carbon:

15. Draw a covalent bonding for water, carbon dioxide, and ammonia.

IONS

16. An atom becomes an ion when it gains or loses one or more _____ .

17. The sodium ion has (*gained, lost*) one electron and is called a(n) (*anion, cation*).

POLAR MOLECULES

18. Describe a polar bond.

19. The electric charge associated with a polar bond is (*greater, lesser*) than the charge of a fully ionized atom.

20. Differentiate between polar and nonpolar molecules.

Hydrogen Bonds

21. Describe a hydrogen bond.

Water

22. Describe the type of bond in a water molecule. Compare with the type of bond that attracts water molecules to each other.

SOLUTIONS

23. Differentiate among a solute, solvent, and solution.

24. The most abundant solvent in the body is _____ .

Molecular Solubility

25. Describe an ionic bond.

26. Differentiate between hydrophilic and hydrophobic molecules.

27. Amphipathic molecules have a(n) _____ region at one end of the molecule and a(n) _____ region at the opposite end.

Concentration

28. The concentration of a substance in solution is defined as:

29. The molecular weight of a molecule is defined as:

30. The mole of a compound is defined as:

31. A solution containing 45 g of glucose in 1 L of solution is a(n) _____ M glucose solution.

Hydrogen Ions and Acidity

32. Molecules that release hydrogen ions into solution are called _____, while substances that accept hydrogen ions are called _____ .

33. (*Strong, weak*) acids or bases completely ionize in solution, while (*strong, weak*) acids or bases do not completely ionize in solution.

34. The relationship between pH and hydrogen-ion concentration expressed in a formula is:

35. The pH of solution A with a hydrogen-ion concentration of 1×10^{-5} M is _____, while the pH of solution B with a hydrogen-ion concentration of 1×10^{-9} M is _____. Solution A is more (*acidic, basic*) than solution B.

36. As acidity increases, pH (*increases, decreases*).

37. The normal range for the pH of body fluids is _____ . This value is slightly (*acidic, basic*).

CLASSES OF ORGANIC MOLECULES

38. The four major categories of organic molecules in the body are:

    a.

    b.

    c.

    d.

Carbohydrates

39. Carbohydrates are composed of the following atoms—_____ , _____ , _____ —in the proportions represented by the following formula:
    _____

40. Differentiate between monosaccharides and disaccharides.

41. Differentiate between pentoses and hexoses.

42. The most abundant monosaccharide in the body is _____ and is stored in cells as the polysaccharide_____ .

Lipids

43. Lipids are composed predominately of the atoms _____ and _____ and lack polar and ionized groups and are therefore (*soluble, insoluble*) in water.

44. The four subclasses of lipids are:

    a.

    b.

    c.

    d.

Fatty acids

45. A fatty acid consists of a long chain of _____ atoms with a _____ group at one end.

46. When all the carbons in a fatty acid chain are linked by single covalent bonds, the fatty acid is said to be (*saturated, unsaturated*).

47. If more than one double bond is present in a fatty acid, that fatty acid is said to be _____.

Triacylglycerols

48. Triacylglycerols are formed by linking together _____ and _____.

49. *Animal fats* contain a high proportion of (*saturated, unsaturated*) fatty acids, whereas *vegetable fats* contain a high proportion of (*saturated, unsaturated*) fatty acids.

Phospholipids

50. Differentiate between a phospholipid and a triacylglycerol.

Steroids

51. The basic structure of all steroids is:

52. Examples of steroids are:

Proteins

53. Proteins are composed primarily of:

54. The smallest unit of a protein is a(n) _____ of which there are _____ different kinds.

55. Two amino acids are linked together by a(n) _____ bond in which the carboxyl group of one amino acid is linked to the amino group of the other and a molecule of _____ is formed.

56. A sequence of amino acids linked together is known as a(n) _____.

57. Monosaccharides attached to specific amino acids in a protein form a class of proteins known as _____.

Primary protein structure

58. Two variables that determine the primary structure of a polypeptide are:

    a.

    b.

Protein conformation

59. Protein conformation refers to:

60. Four factors that determine protein conformation of a polypeptide chain are:

    a.

    b.

    c.

    d.

61. Hydrogen bonds in a peptide chain contribute toward a helical configuration known as a(n) _____ helix.

62. Many proteins contain more than one polypeptide chain. (*true, false*)

Nucleic Acids

63. The two classes of nucleic acids are:

    a.

    b.

Indicate whether the following statements pertain to DNA or to RNA.

64. _____ stores genetic information coded in terms of repeating subunit structure

65. _____ decodes genetic information to link together specific sequences of amino acids to form a specific polypeptide chain

66. _____ contains the nucleotide sugar ribose

67. _____ contains the nucleotide bases cytosine and uracil

68. _____ contains the nucleotide bases cytosine and thymine

69. _____ contains the nucleotide bases adenine and guanine

70. _____ consists of two chains of nucleotides in the form of a double helix

Review the SUMMARY and REVIEW QUESTIONS at the end of this chapter in your textbook.

CHAPTER 2 ANSWER KEY

1. atoms

2. a. protons   b. neutrons   c. electrons

3. a. protons   b. neutrons

4. protons, +1; neutrons, 0 (neutral); electrons, −1

5. nucleus

6. the number of protons in the nucleus

7. protons, neutrons

8. the amount of the element in grams that is equal to the numerical value of its atomic weight

9. hydrogen, oxygen, carbon, nitrogen

10. calcium, phosphorus, potassium, sulfur, sodium, chloride, magnesium

11. two or more atoms bonded together

12. H_2O, $C_6H_{12}O_6$

13. A covalent bond is formed when one electron in the outer electron orbit of each atom is shared between two atoms.

14. a. one   b. two   c. three   d. four

15. H_2O: H—O—H
    CO_2: O=C=O
    NH_3: H—N—H
                |
               H

16. electrons

17. lost, cation

18. A polar bond is a covalent bond in which the electrons are not shared equally between the two atoms; one atom acquires a lightly negative charge, while the other atom has a slightly positive charge.

19. lesser

20. Polar molecules contain a significant number of polar bonds or ionized groups. Nonpolar molecules are composed predominately of electrically neutral bonds.

21. A hydrogen bond (a weak bond) is the electric attraction between a hydrogen atom in one polarized bond and an oxygen or nitrogen atom in a polarized bond of another molecule (or within the same molecule if the bonds are sufficiently separated from each other).

22. There are polarized covalent bonds between the hydrogen and oxygen atoms in a water molecule and hydrogen bonds between adjacent water molecules.

23. Solute is a substance that is dissolved in a liquid. Solvent is the liquid in which a solute is dissolved. Solution includes the solvent and solute.

24. water (60 percent or more of total body weight)

25. An ionic bond is a strong bond between two oppositely charged ions.

26. Hydrophilic molecules have a large number of polar bonds and/or ionized groups and easily dissolve in water (water-loving molecules). Hydrophobic molecules have predominately electrically neutral covalent bonds and are insoluble in water (water-fearing molecules).

27. polar or ionized, nonpolar

28. the amount of the solute present in a unit volume of solution (example: gm/L or mole/L)

29. the sum of the atomic weights of all the atoms in the molecule (examples: H_2O: 2[1] + 16 = 18; $C_6H_{12}O_6$: 6[12] + 12[1] + 6[16] = 180)

30. the amount of the compound in grams equal to its molecular weight

31. 0.25

32. acids, bases

33. strong, weak

34. $pH = -\log[H^+]$

35. 5, 9, acidic

36. decreases

37. 7.35 to 7.45, basic

38. a. carbohydrates   b. lipids   c. proteins   d. nucleic acids

39. C, H, O, $C_n(H_2O)_n$

40. Monosaccharides are the simplest sugars, having five or six carbons. An example of a six-carbon sugar is glucose, and an example of a five-carbon sugar is fructose. Disaccharides are composed of two monosaccharides. An example is sucrose, composed of glucose and fructose.

41. Pentoses are monosaccharides containing five-carbon atoms. Hexoses are monosaccharides containing six-carbon atoms.

42. glucose, glycogen

43. C, H, insoluble

44. a. fatty acids   b. triacylglycerols   c. phospholipids   d. steroids

45. C, carboxyl

46. saturated

47. polyunsaturated

48. glycerol, three fatty acids

49. saturated, unsaturated

50. A tricylglycerol has three fatty acid chains attached to a glycerol molecule, whereas a phospholipid has two fatty acid chains attached to a glycerol molecule with the third group being a phosphate group with a polar nitrogen-containing molecule.

51. four interconnected rings of carbon atoms (See Fig. 2-12, page 27.)

52. cholesterol, cortisol, estrogen, progesterone, testosterone

53. carbon, hydrogen, oxygen, nitrogen, sulfur

54. amino acid, 20

55. peptide, water (See Fig. 2-14, page 29.)

56. polypeptide

57. glycoproteins

58. a. the number of amino acids in the chain
    b. the specific type of amino acid at each position along the chain

59. the three-dimensional shape of the protein

60. a. hydrogen bonds   c. van der Waals forces
    b. ionic bonds   d. covalent bonds

(See Fig. 2–17, page 32 and Table 2–6, page 33.)

61. alpha

62. true

63. a. deoxyribonucleic acid (DNA)   b. ribonucleic acid (RNA

64. DNA

65. RNA

66. RNA

67. RNA

68. DNA

69. DNA and RNA

70. DNA

CHAPTER
3
CELL STRUCTURE

MICROSCOPIC OBSERVATIONS OF CELLS

1. The smallest objects (diameter) that can be seen with the following are:

   a. Human eye:

   b. Light microscope:

   c. Electron microscope:

2. Explain why living cells cannot be observed with an electron microscope.

3. Differentiate between eukaryotic cells, prokaryotic cells, and viruses. Give examples of each.

   a. Eukaryotic cells:

   b. Prokaryotic cells:

   c. Viruses:

CELL COMPARTMENTS

4. The two major divisions inside a cell are:

   a.

   b.

5. The two components of the cytoplasm are:

   a.

   b.

6. Differentiate between cytoplasm and cytosol.

Membranes

7. The major function of biological membranes is:

Membrane structure

8. Describe the arrangement of lipids and proteins in a membrane.

9. Carbohydrates linked to membrane lipids and proteins form a layer known as the
   _____ .

Membrane junctions

10. Three types of membrane junctions that link adjacent cells are _____,
    _____ , and _____.

11. Illustrate how each of the membrane junctions listed in question 10 appears between two adjacent cells.

12. Indicate which type of membrane junction is best described by the following:

    a. _____ hold adjacent cells firmly together in areas that are subject to considerable stretching, such as the skin
    b. _____ form channels between the cytoplasm of adjacent cells and play an important role in the transmission of electrical activity between certain types of muscle cells
    c. _____ found primarily in epithelial cells, and limit the movement of molecules through the extracellular space between cells

CELL ORGANELLES

Nucleus

13. The primary function of the nucleus is:

14. Draw a nucleus, illustrating the nuclear envelope, nuclear pores, nucleolus, and chromatin.

15. Chromatin threads are composed of:

16. The nucleolus is composed of:

Ribosomes

17. The major function of the ribosome is _____ .

Endoplasmic Reticulum

18. The two types of endoplasmic reticulum and the function of each are:

    a.

    b.

Golgi Apparatus

19. The Golgi apparatus is a series of closely opposed, flattened membranous sacs that sort _____ synthesized on the rough endoplasmic reticulum and package them into secretory vesicles.

Mitochondria

20. Draw a mitochondrion. Label the outer and inner membranes, matrix, and cristae.

21. Mitochondria are the major sites of _____ production.

Lysosomes

22. Lysosomes are spherical or oval organelles whose primary function is:

Peroxisomes

23. Peroxisomes are oval organelles whose primary function is:

Filaments

24. The four classes of filaments that are involved in the cell's cytoskeleton are:

    a.

    b.

    c.

    d.

Review the SUMMARY and REVIEW QUESTIONS at the end of this chapter in your textbook.

CHAPTER 3 ANSWER KEY

1. 100 μm, 0.2 μm, 0.002 μm

2. Cells must be specially prepared for observation using an electron microscope by being cut into very thin sections (approx. 0.1 μm thick = approx. 1/100 the thickness of a typical cell). Therefore, the cells are not *sections*, not *living* cells.

3.   a.   eukaryotic cells: cells which have a true nucleus with a nuclear membrane and numerous membrane-bound organelles (example: all cells of the human body)
     b.   prokaryotic cells: cells which do not have a defined nucleus or membrane-bound organelles (example: bacteria)
     c.   viruses: have only a nucleic acid molecule surrounded by a protein shell

4.   a.   nucleus   b.   cytoplasm

5.   a.   cell organelles   b.   cytosol

6. Cytoplasm contains all of the cell contents except for the nucleus, whereas the cytosol is the liquid that fills all the cytoplasmic region except the interior of the cell organelles.

7. to regulate movement of molecules and ions into and out of cells and cell organelles

8. There is a double layer of lipid molecules (the bimolecular lipid layer) composed of phospholipids and cholesterol. This lipid layer is very fluid, making the membrane very flexible. Embedded in this lipid layer are two classes of proteins: integral proteins which span the entire membrane, and peripheral membrane proteins which are primarily located on the cytoplasmic surface of the plasma membrane.

9. glycocalyx

10. desmosomes, tight junctions, gap junctions

11. See Fig. 3-9, page 49.

12.   a.   desmosome   b.   gap junction   c.   tight junction

13. storage, transmission, and expression of genetic information in protein synthesis

14. See Fig. 3-10, page 51.

15. DNA and proteins

16. RNA and proteins

17. protein synthesis

18. a. granular (rough-surfaced): has ribosomes attached to the membranes which are involved in protein packaging
    b. agranular (smooth-surfaced): lacks ribosomes, is site of synthesis of lipid molecules and also stores and releases calcium ions involved in controlling cell activities

19. proteins

20. See Fig. 3-13, page 54.

21. ATP

22. digestion of particulate matter that enters a cell

23. breaking down certain toxic products formed from oxygen

24. a. microfilaments (actin)
    b. intermediate filaments
    c. thick filaments (myosin)
    d. microtubules

CHAPTER
4
MOLECULAR CONTROL MECHANISMS: PROTEINS AND DNA

Section A. Binding Sites On Proteins

BINDING-SITE CHARACTERISTICS

1. A molecule or ion that binds to a specific site on a protein is known as a _____ , and the specific site to which it binds on the protein is known as a _____ .

Match:

2. ___ the ability of a protein to bind to a specific ligand

3. ___ the strength of the ligand-protein binding at a binding site

4. ___ the fraction of binding sites that are occupied at any given time

5. ___ more than one type of ligand may bind to certain binding sites

    a. affinity

    b. chemical specificity

    c. competition

    d. percent saturation

6. High-affinity binding sites are those at which ligands are tightly bound to the binding sites. (*true, false*)

7. Illustrate how three different binding sites can have the same chemical affinity for a ligand but have different affinities.

8. The percent saturation of a binding site depends upon:

   a.

   b.

9. Increasing the ligand concentration increases the number of binding sites occupied. At 100 percent saturation of the binding sites, further increases in ligand concentration do not increase the saturation of the binding sites. Show how such a curve for the above situation would look on this *X-Y* axis.

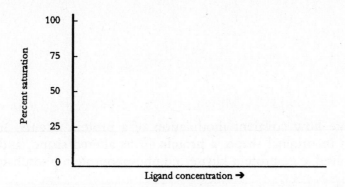

10. On the graph below, draw a curve representing a protein with a low-affinity binding site (*X*) for a ligand, and a curve representing a protein with a high-affinity binding site (*Y*) for the same ligand.

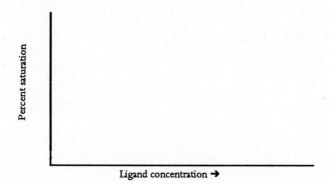

On the graph above, indicate with the letter (B) the ligand concentration for the low-affinity binding protein which represents 50 percent saturation. Indicate with the letter (A) the ligand concentration for the high-affinity binding protein which represents 50 percent saturation.

REGULATION OF BINDING-SITE CHARACTERISTICS

11. Two mechanisms that are used by cells to selectively alter protein shape are:

    a.

    b.

12. Describe or illustrate how allosteric modulation of a protein occurs. Include the allosteric protein, regulatory site, functional site, modulator molecule, and ligand.

13. Describe or illustrate how covalent modulation of a protein occurs. Include the ligand, a protein in its original shape, a protein in its altered shape, and a specific enzyme system involved, e.g., protein kinase and phosphoprotein phosphatase.

Review the SUMMARY and REVIEW QUESTIONS at the end of this section in your textbook.

Section B. Genetic Information and Protein Synthesis

GENETIC INFORMATION

14. Differentiate between a gene and a genome.

Match:

15. ____ genes with identical nucleotide sequences

16. ____ genes with slightly different nucleotide sequences

17. ____ variants of the same gene

a. allele
b. dominant gene
c. heterozygous
d. homozygous
e. recessive gene

18. Describe how the information contained in DNA is expressed in protein synthesis.

19. The four bases in a DNA molecule are _____, _____, _____, and _____.

20. A three-base sequence that specifies a particular amino acid is known as a(n) _____ .

21. A three-base sequence that indicates the end of a genetic message is known as a(n) _____.

PROTEIN SYNTHESIS

22. Passing genetic information from DNA to mRNA in the nucleus is known as _____ .

23. Passing genetic information from mRNA in the nucleus to the cytoplasm for protein synthesis is known as _____ .

Transcription: mRNA Synthesis

24. The base in RNA that differs from the bases in DNA is _____.

25. The bases in an exposed DNA nucleotide sequence are C, G, and A. Complementary bases in the mRNA sequence would be (in order): _____.

26. The enzyme which must be bound to DNA for its activity and which joins together the ribonucleotides of the transcribed mRNA is _____.

27. Which of the two DNA strands is used as a template for mRNA synthesis?

28. A three-base sequence in mRNA that specifies one amino acid is known as (an) _____.

29. Expressed regions of a gene are known as _____ , and noncoding, intervening sequences are known as _____ .

30. While the mRNA is still in the nucleus, it is processed (spliced) to remove all the (*exons, introns*).

Translation: Polypeptide Synthesis

31. Processed mRNA moves from the nucleus to the cytoplasm where one end of the mRNA binds to an organelle called the _____.

32. The type of RNA that combines with both a specific amino acid and a codon in mRNA specific for that amino acid is _____.

33. _____ is the enzyme that links a specific amino acid to a particular type of tRNA.

34. The three-nucleotide sequence at the end of one of the loops of tRNA, called the _____, can base-pair with the complementary codon on the mRNA.

Protein assembly

35. The individual amino acids linked to mRNA by tRNA are bound to each other by _____ bonds.

36. A completed protein chain is released from the ribosome when the _____ codon in mRNA is reached.

Protein Secretion

37. If a signal sequence (the first 15 to 30 amino acids) is present on a growing polypeptide chain, protein synthesis may be continued on the _____.

Regulation of Protein Synthesis

38. _____ facilitate the RNA polymerase binding to promote genes.

39. Factors that regulate the rate of protein synthesis are:

    a.

    b.

    c.

    d.

REPLICATION AND EXPRESSION OF GENETIC INFORMATION

Replication of DNA

40. Briefly describe DNA replication.

Cell Division

41. The time period between the end of one cell division and the appearance of structural changes indicating the beginning of the next division is known as _____ .

42. Differentiate among the G_1, S, and G_2 phases of the cell cycle.

    G_1 (first gap):

    S (synthesis):

    G_2 (second gap):

43. The two processes of cell division are:

    a.

    b.

44. DNA replication occurs during _____, forming two identical sister chromatids joined by a(n) _____ .

45. Chromatids become highly coiled and condensed into chromosomes as the cell enters _____ .

46. _____ connect the two centrioles with the centromeres of the chromo-somes.

47. The sister chromatids in each chromosome separate at the _____ and move toward the opposite centrioles. (*One, two, three, four*) new daughter cells form.

48. Place these events in proper time sequence: G_0, G_1, G_2, M, S, cytokinesis.

49. What is the function of cell division cycle (cdc) genes?

Mutation

50. Proofreading for errors in duplication of DNA is largely the responsibility of the enzyme _____.

51. Define:
    Mutation:

    Mutagen:

52. Types of mutations that can occur are:
    a.

    b.

53. The range of severity of the effect of mutations on cell functions includes:
    a.

    b.

    c.

54. DNA repair mechanisms utilizing DNA polymerase require that one of the two DNA strands be undamaged to provide the correct code for rebuilding the damaged strand. (*true/false*)

Recombinant DNA

55. What is recombinant DNA?

56. What are potential advantages in using recombinant DNA technology?

CANCER

Match:

57. ___ dominant cancer-producing genes

58. ___ genes that prevent cancerous transformations produced by oncogenes

59. ___ spread of cancerous cells to other parts of the body

60. ___ cancers derived from connective tissue and muscle

61. ___ cancers that develop in epithelial cells

62. ___ cancers that develop from blood cells

a. carcinomas
b. leukemias
c. metastasis
d. oncogenes
e. sarcomas
f. tumor suppressor genes

Review the SUMMARY and REVIEW QUESTIONS at the end of this section and the THOUGHT QUESTIONS at the end of this chapter in your textbook.

34 ◆ Chapter 4

CHAPTER 4 ANSWER KEY

1. ligand, binding site

2. b

3. a

4. d

5. c

6. true

7. See Fig. 4-4, page 60.

8. a. the concentration of the unbound ligand in the solution
   b. the affinity of the binding site for the ligand

9. See Fig. 4-5, page 61.

10. See Fig. 4-6, page 61.

11. a. allosteric modulation
    b. covalent modulation

12. See Fig. 4-7A, page 63.

13. See Fig. 4-7B, page 63.

14. A gene is a sequence of nucleotides containing information that determines the amino acid sequence of a single polypeptide chain—a unit of hereditary information. A genome is the total collection of genes that specifies a particular organism's structure and function. The human genome has between 50,000 and 100,000 genes.

15. d

16. c

17. a

18. DNA located in the nucleus is transcribed into RNA in the nucleus followed by translation of the RNA into protein synthesis in the cytoplasm.

19. adenine (A), guanine (G), cytosine (C), thymine (T)

20. triplet code

21. termination code

23. translation

24. uracil (It is present in place of thymine.)

25. G, C, and U

26. RNA polymerase

27. The DNA strand which has a promoter base sequence for binding DNA polymerase, a specific sequence of nucleotides in DNA, is present in only one of the two DNA strands. DNA polymerase binds to the promoter and moves along one strand, forming an mRNA strand. (See Fig. 4–10, page 67.)

28. codon

29. exons, introns

30. introns

31. ribosome

32. tRNA

33. aminoacyl-tRNA synthetase

34. anticodon

35. peptide

36. termination

37. endoplasmic reticulum

38. transcription factors

39. a. DNA transcription into mRNA
    b. splicing of mRNA
    c. stability of mRNA
    d. translation of mRNA by ribosomes

40. The two strands of the DNA double helix separate, and the exposed bases in each strand base-pair with free deoxyribonucleotide triphosphates present in the nucleus. DNA polymerase links the free nucleotides together to form a complementary copy.

41. interphase

42. G_1 (first gap): period from the end of cell division to the beginning of the S phase
    S (synthesis): periods of replication of DNA, usually lasting about 7 h
    G_2 (second gap): period following the end of DNA synthesis before the physical signs of cell division begin

43. a. mitosis (nuclear division)   b. cytokinesis (cytoplasmic division)

44. interphase, centromere

45. mitosis

46. spindle fibers

47. centromere, two

48. G_1, S, G_2, M, cytokinesis, G_0

49. Cdc (cell division cycle) genes code for specific protein kinase enzymes that are essential for progression through the G_1 to S phase and G_2 to M phase.

50. DNA polymerase

51. Mutation: an alteration in the genetic message carried by DNA
    Mutagen: a factor that induces or increases mutation rates in DNA

52. a. incorrect base(s) inserted into new strands of DNA
    b. single bases added or deleted or large sections of DNA deleted

53. a. no noticeable effect on cell functioning
    b. modification of cell functioning but compatible with cell growth and replication
    c. cell death

54. true

55. Recombinant DNA is the segments of DNA cut from one cell using bacterial enzymes which are inserted into the DNA of another cell. This new recombinant DNA is then incorporated into directing the functions of the new cell.

56. Recombinant DNA technology may provide us with the ability to selectively replace mutant genes with normal genes and possibly provide a cure for genetic diseases.

57. d

58. f

59. c

60. e

61. a

62. b

CHAPTER
5
ENERGY AND CELLULAR METABOLISM

1. Differentiate among metabolism, anabolism, and catabolism.

CHEMICAL REACTIONS

2. Chemical reactions involve the following two processes:

   a.

   b.

3. What happens to the energy content of the reactants and products during chemical reactions?

4. Energy that is released during a chemical reaction is measured in a unit called a(n) _____ , which is defined as:

Determinants of Reaction Rates

5. Four factors that influence chemical reaction rates are:

   a.

   b.

   c.

   d.

6. If there is an <u>increase</u> in each of the above factors, will there be an increase (I) or a decrease (D) in the <u>reaction rate</u>?

   a.

   b.

   c.

   d.

Reversible and Irreversible Reactions

7. Write a word equation using the following terms: reactants, products, forward reaction, and reverse reactions.

8. Does the above word equation represent a reversible or an irreversible reaction?

9. List the characteristics of reversible and irreversible reactions.

   Reversible reactions:

   a.

   b.

   Irreversible reactions:

   a.

   b.

Law of Mass Action

10. Define the law of mass action.

ENZYMES

11. List important characteristics of an enzyme.

    a.

    b.

12. A typical cell contains approximately _____ different enzymes.

13. An enzyme usually ends with the suffix _____ .

Cofactors

14. Define cofactor.

15. Examples of cofactors are:

REGULATION OF ENZYME-MEDIATED REACTIONS

16. The rate of an enzyme-mediated reaction depends on:

    a.

    b.

    c.

Substrate Concentration

17. On the *X-Y* axis below, indicate how an enzyme-catalyzed reaction is affected by an increase in substrate concentration.

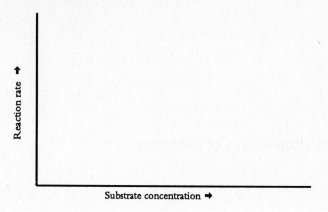

18. Indicate on the graph above the substrate concentration at which the enzyme is saturated.

Enzyme Concentration

19. On the *X-Y* axis below, indicate how an enzyme-catalyzed reaction is affected by an increase in substrate concentration at two enzyme concentrations—A and 2A—with 2A twice the enzyme concentration A, producing twice the reaction rate.

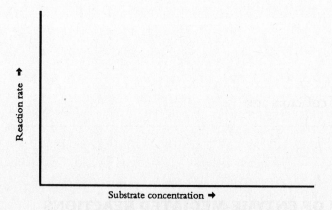

Enzyme Activity

20. On the *X-Y* axis below, indicate how an enzyme-catalyzed reaction is affected by an increase in the affinity of an enzyme for its substrate by allosteric or covalent modulation. (Show the normal affinity of the enzyme for the substrate and the increased affinity of the enzyme for the substrate.)

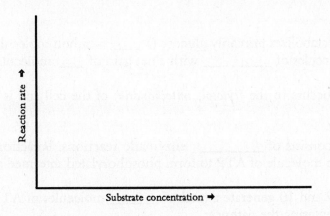

MULTIENZYME METABOLIC PATHWAYS

21. On the diagram below, indicate a rate-limiting enzyme (E) and end-product inhibi-
    tion (I). Draw a broken line representing allosteric inhibition of E.

$$A \underset{}{\overset{e_1}{\rightleftharpoons}} B \underset{}{\overset{e_2}{\rightleftharpoons}} C \underset{}{\overset{e_3}{\rightleftharpoons}} D \overset{e_4}{\longrightarrow} E$$

ATP AND CELLULAR ENERGY TRANSFER

The Role of ATP

22. When 1 mol of ATP is hydrolyzed to ADP, _____ kcal of energy is released.

23. Cells use ATP to (*transfer, store*) energy.

24. ATP is generated from three metabolic pathways:

    a.

    b.

    c.

25. In the catabolism (breakdown) of fuel molecules, ____percent of the energy released
    is in the form of ATP and ____ percent is in the form of heat.

26. Complete these reactions:

    a. ATP + _____ → ADP + _____ + _____

    b. ADP + _____ + _____ → ATP + _____

Glycolysis

27. Glycolysis catabolizes primarily glucose (a _____ -carbon molecule) into _____ three-carbon molecules of _____ with a net gain of ____ molecules of ATP.

28. Glycolysis occurs in the (*cytosol, mitochondria*) of the cell and is an (*aerobic, anaerobic*) process.

29. Glycolysis consists of _____ enzymatic reactions. Reactions 1 and 3 each (*use, produce*) one molecule of ATP to form phosphorylated intermediates.

30. Reactions 7 and 10 generate a total of _____ molecules of ATP for every molecule of glucose entering the pathway.

31. The *net gain* of ATP during glycolysis is therefore _____ molecules formed by _____ level phosphorylation.

32. Under aerobic conditions, pyruvate is converted to _____ via the _____ , but under anaerobic conditions, pyruvate is converted to _____ .

33. Examples in which glycolysis supplies most of the cell's ATP are _____ because these cells lack _____ .

Krebs Cycle

34. Most of the enzymes for the Krebs cycle are located in _____ .

35. Two other names for the Krebs cycle are:

    a.

    b.

36. The primary molecule entering the Krebs cycle is _____, which can come from pyruvate or from the breakdown of fatty acids. Pyruvate + CoA + $NAD^+ \rightarrow$ _____ + _____ + NADH + H^+.

37. The two-carbon molecule, _____, is transferred to the four-carbon molecule, _____, to form the six-carbon molecule, _____ .

38. One molecule of _____ is given off in the third step and one molecule in the fourth step of the Krebs cycle.

39. ATP is formed from _____ in the Krebs cycle.

40. During one rotation of the Krebs cycle _____ molecule(s) of carbon dioxide is (are) produced, ____ pair(s) of hydrogen atoms is (are) transferred to coenzymes, and ____ molecule(s) of GTP is (are) formed by substrate-level phosphorylation which can be converted to ATP.

Oxidative Phosphorylation

41. During oxidative phosphorylation, energy to form ATP is derived from energy released when hydrogen combines with _____ to form _____ and _____ kcal/mol of energy.

42. The enzymes for oxidative phosphorylation are located in _____ .

43. Important electron transport proteins in the electron transport chain are known as _____ .

44. Discuss the chemiosmotic hypothesis by which ATP is formed by means of the electron transport chain.

45. The majority of ATP is formed by _____ in the cell organelles known as _____ .

CARBOHYDRATE, FAT, AND PROTEIN METABOLISM

Carbohydrate catabolism

46. Complete the following reaction:
    $C_6H_{12}O_6 + 6\ O_2 \rightarrow$ _____ + _____ + _____

47. Under aerobic conditions one molecule of glucose forms
    __ molecule(s) of ATP
    __ molecule(s) of ATP from glycolysis
    __ molecule(s) of ATP from the Krebs cycle
    __ molecule(s) of ATP from oxidative phosphorylation

48. Under anaerobic conditions, one molecule of glucose forms ___ molecule(s) of ATP.

Glycogen storage

49. Excess glucose can be stored as glycogen in _____ and _____ .

50. Glycogen can be broken down into _____ and used as a source of cellular energy. _____ glycogen can also be broken down into glucose and thus leave the cell and enter the blood.

Glucose synthesis

51. The process of generating new glucose from nonglucose precursors (glycerol, lactic acid, some amino acids) is called _____ . This process occurs primarily in the _____ and _____ .

Fat Metabolism

Fat catabolism

52. Fat accounts for approximately ____ percent of the energy stored in the body.

53. Body fat is stored in specialized cells known as _____ .

54. The enzymes for fatty acid catabolism are located in the _____ . These enzymes break down fatty acid chains by _____ (two carbons at a time) to form acetyl coenzyme A and hydrogen atoms.

55. The catabolism of one 18-carbon saturated fatty acid yields _____ ATP molecule(s). The catabolism of one six-carbon glucose yields a maximum of ___ ATP molecule(s).

Fat synthesis

56. Fatty acids are synthesized from _____ by enzymes located in the _____ of the cell.

57. Fatty acids are linked to _____ to form triacylglycerol by enzymes associated with the membranes of the _____ .

Protein and Amino Acid Metabolism

58. The enzymes that break down proteins into free amino acids are _____ .

59. The two ways in which the amino group can be removed from an amino acid are:

    a.

    b.

60. Oxidative deamination of amino acids results in the production of _____ which is converted to _____ by the liver and excreted by the_____.

61. Define essential amino acids.

62. A net loss of amino acids over a period of time is known as a(n) _____, while a net gain of amino acids is known as a(n) _____.

Fuel Metabolism Summary

Review Fig. 5-24, page 111.

ESSENTIAL NUTRIENTS

63. Two criteria for substances to be listed as "essential nutrients" are:

a.

b.

64. _____ of the 20 amino acids and _____ of the fatty acids are "essential nutrients."

65. List some of the other 50 essential nutrients.

Vitamins

66. Differentiate between water-soluble and fat-soluble vitamins.

Review the SUMMARY, REVIEW QUESTIONS, and THOUGHT QUESTIONS at the end of this chapter in your textbook.

CHAPTER 5 ANSWER KEY

1. Metabolism is all the chemical reactions occurring continuously. Anabolism is the synthesis of organic molecules. Catabolism is the breakdown of organic molecules.

2. a. breaking of chemical bonds in the reactant molecules
   b. making of new bonds to form the product molecules

3. Since energy can neither be created nor destroyed, it is either added or released during a chemical reaction.

4. calories. One calorie is the amount of heat required to raise the temperature of 1 g of water 1°C.

5. a. reactant concentration
   b. activation energy
   c. temperature
   d. presence of a catalyst

6. a. I   b. D   c. I   d. I

7. Reactants $\underset{\substack{\text{Reverse}\\\text{reaction}}}{\overset{\substack{\text{Forward}\\\text{reaction}}}{\rightleftharpoons}}$ Products

8. Reversible

9. Reversible reactions:
   a. Only a small amount of energy is released or added during the reaction.
   b. At chemical equilibrium, product concentrations are only slightly higher than reactant concentrations.
   Irreversible reactions:
   a. A large amount of energy is released or added during the reaction.
   b. At chemical equilibrium, almost all reactant molecules have been converted to product.

10. The law of mass action is the effect of increasing or decreasing the reactant or product concentrations on the direction in which the net reaction will proceed.

11. a. An enzyme lowers the activation energy required for a reaction but does not cause any reaction to occur that would not occur in its absence.
    b. The enzyme binds with the substrate at the active site to accelerate the reaction rate but does not undergo chemical change itself. (See Table 5-3, page 89.)

12. 4000

13. -ase

14. A cofactor is a substance which in small concentrations activates an enzyme.

15. trace metals (iron, zinc, copper, etc.), coenzymes (NAD^+ and FAD)

16. a. substrate concentration
    b. enzyme concentration
    c. enzyme activity

17. See Fig. 5-3, page 91.

18. Note vertical saturation line in Fig. 5-3, page 91.

19. See Fig. 5-4, page 91.

20. See Fig. 5-5, page 91.

21.

$$
\begin{array}{c}
\quad\quad\quad\quad\quad E \swarrow \quad\quad\quad\quad I \\
e_1 \quad\quad e_2 \quad E_3 \quad\quad e_4 \searrow \\
\text{A} \quad \text{B} \quad\quad \text{C} \quad\quad \text{D} \quad\quad \text{E}
\end{array}
$$

22. 7

23. transfer

24. a. glycolysis
    b. Krebs cycle
    c. oxidative phosphorylation

25. 40, 60

26. a. H_2O, P_i, 7 kcal/mol
    b. P_i, 7 kcal/mol, H_2O

27. six, two pyruvate, two

28. cytosol, anaerobic

29. 10, use

30. four

31. two, substrate

32. CO_2, ATP, and H^+; Krebs cycle; lactate

33. erythrocytes (red blood cells) and certain types of skeletal-muscle cells, mitochondria

34. the mitochondria (inner membrane)

35. a. citric acid cycle
    b. tricarboxylic acid cycle

36. acetyl coenzyme A, acetyl CoA, CO_2

37. acetyl CoA, oxaloacetate, citrate

38. CO_2

39. GTP

40. two, four, one

41. oxygen, water, 53

42. the mitochondria (inner membrane)

43. cytochromes

44. As electrons pass along the cytochrome chain, hydrogen ions are moved from the matrix to the cytosol side of the inner mitochondrial membrane (a source of potential energy), forming a hydrogen-ion gradient across the membrane. At three points along the electron transport chain, channels are present through which the hydrogen ions can flow back to the matrix side from the cytoplasmic side in the mitochondria and transfer their potential energy to the formation of ATP from ADP and P_i.

45. oxidative phosphorylation, mitochondria

46. 6 H_2O, 6 CO_2, 686 kcal/mol

47. 38, 2, 2, 34

48. two

49. liver, skeletal muscle

50. glucose-6-phosphate, liver

51. gluconeogenesis, kidney, liver

52. 80

53. adipocytes

54. mitochondrial matrix, beta oxidation

55. 146, 38

56. acetyl coenzyme A, cytosol

57. α-glycerolphosphate, smooth endoplasmic reticulum

58. proteases

59. a. oxidative deamination
    b. transamination

60. ammonia, urea, kidneys

61. Essential amino acids are the nine amino acids that cannot be synthesized by the body and must be present in our diet.

62. negative nitrogen balance, positive nitrogen balance

63. a. They must not be synthesized by the body in adequate amounts.
    b. They must be essential for health.

64. 9, 2

65. See Table 5-10, page 112.

66. Water-soluble vitamins form portions of coenzymes and include the B complex and C. Since they are water-soluble, they can be excreted in the urine if ingested in excess. Fat-soluble vitamins do not function as coenzymes in general. They include A, D, E, and K. Since they are fat-soluble, they are stored in fat tissue and therefore may be toxic if taken in excess.

CHAPTER
6
MOVEMENT OF MOLECULES
ACROSS CELL MEMBRANES

DIFFUSION

1. Define diffusion and give an example of a substance that moves by diffusion in a living organism.

Magnitude and Direction of Diffusion

2. The amount of material crossing a surface per unit time is known as _____.

3. The three fluxes at any surface where a concentration gradient exists and a permeable membrane is present are:

   a.

   b.

   c.

4. The greater the difference in concentration of molecules on two sides of a permeable membrane, the (*greater, lesser*) the net flux.

5. Net flux will increase (I), decrease (D), or not change (NC) for the following situations:
   a. _____ an increase in temperature
   b. _____ an increase in mass (size) of the molecules
   c. _____ an increase in surface area available for diffusion

Diffusion through Membranes

6. The equation for the net flux across a permeable membrane is:

7. Define each factor in the above equation.

8. What is occurring if there is a negative net flux value?

Diffusion through the lipid bilayer

9. (*Polar, nonpolar*) molecules have a higher lipid solubility and diffuse through the lipid bilayer of biological membranes more rapidly. Examples of this kind of molecule are:

Diffusion of ions through protein channels

10. Draw a hypothetical diagram illustrating protein channels in a biological membrane through which ions diffuse.

Role of electric forces on ion movements

11. Define what is meant by the electrochemical gradient across a membrane.

Regulation of diffusion through membranes

12. The process of opening and closing ion channels is known as _____ .

13. Three types of channels that may be present (even for the same ion) include:

   a.

   b.

   c.

MEDIATED-TRANSPORT SYSTEMS

14. Diagram a model of a carrier-mediated transport system.

15. Approximately _____ percent of the total membrane proteins are transport proteins.

16. Three factors that determine the magnitude of the net flux through a mediated transport system are:

   a.

   b.

   c.

17. On the graph below, draw a line indicating the flux of molecules across a membrane due to diffusion and draw a line indicating a mediated-transport system. Label each.

Flux into cell →

Extracellular solute concentration →

18. Two types of mediated transport are:

    a.

    b.

Facilitated Diffusion

19. Define facilitated diffusion.

20. Differentiate between diffusion and facilitated diffusion on the graphs below.

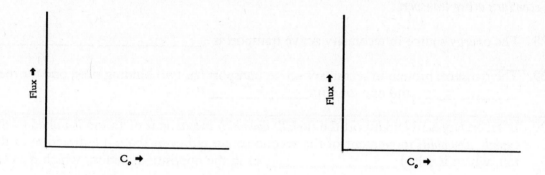

21. An example of a substance that moves by facilitated diffusion is _____.

Active Transport

22. Define active transport.

23. The source of energy for active transport is from _____.

24. Two ways of coupling energy to transport proteins are:

    a.

    b.

Primary active transport

25. In primary active transport,_____, an ATPase, catalyzes the breakdown of ATP and phosphorylates itself.

26. Four identified transport proteins involved in ion transport are:

    a.

    b.

    c.

    d.

27. For each molecule of ATP hydrolyzed, the Na^+,K^+-ATPase moves _____ sodium ion(s) (*into, out of*) a cell and _____ potassium ion(s) (*into, out of*) a cell.

Secondary active transport

28. The energy source in secondary active transport is _____ .

29. The transport protein in secondary active transport has two binding sites, one for the _____ and one for a(n) _____ .

30. In secondary active transport the (*uphill, downhill*) movement of an ion is linked to the (*uphill, downhill*) movement of the second solute either in the same direction as the ion, which is called _____, or in the opposite direction, which is called _____ .

31. An example of an organic molecule cotransported across a biological membrane by sodium-coupled secondary active transport is a(n) _____ .

32. An example of an ion countertransported across a biological membrane by a sodium-coupled secondary active transport is _____ .

Review Table 6-2, page 135.

OSMOSIS

33. Define osmosis.

34. What is the molarity (*M*) of 1 L of water?

35. Adding a solute to 1 L of water will (*increase, decrease*) the water concentration.

36. Indicate how many times the water concentration would be decreased by the addition of 1 mol of the following as compared to the addition of 1 mol of glucose.

    a. Sodium chloride (NaCl):

    b. Magnesium chloride ($MgCl_2$):

    c. Calcium chloride ($CaCl_2$):

    d. An amino acid:

    e. A fatty acid:

    f. Urea:

37. The total solute concentration in a solution is known as its _____ .

38. One osmole equals _____ of solute particles.

39. A 2 *M* solution of glucose is equal to an osmolarity of _____ , while a 2 *M* solution of calcium chloride is equal to an osmolarity of _____ .

40. Draw a diagram showing two compartments separated by a membrane permeable to solute and water which has a greater solute concentration on one side than the other. Diagram the net diffusion of water and solute and indicate if there is a volume change in the compartments.

41. Draw a diagram showing two compartments separated by a membrane permeable to water but not to the solute which has a greater solute concentration on one side than the other. Diagram the net diffusion of water and solute and indicate if there is a volume change.

42. Differentiate between osmolarity and osmotic pressure.

43. The greater the osmolarity of a solution, the (*greater, lesser*) the osmotic pressure.

Extracellular Osmolarity and Cell Volume

44. The major nonpenetrating solutes outside the cell are _____ and _____ , and inside the cell, _____ and _____.

45. The osmolarity of the extracellular and intracellular fluid is about _____ mOsmol/L.

46. If living cells are placed in a solution that has more than 300 mOsmol/L of non-penetrating solute, the cells will (*shrink, swell, stay the same volume*). A solution such as this is said to be _____ .

47. A solution which causes living cells to swell is known as a(n) _____ solution. The net flux of water in this situation is:

48. If cells are placed in a solution in which there is no net change in cell volume, that solution is known as a(n) _____ solution.

49. Differentiate between an isosmotic and an isotonic solution.

50. Intravenous solutions introduced into individuals for administration of drugs, volume replacement, etc., are (*hypotonic, isotonic, hypertonic*). Why?

ENDOCYTOSIS AND EXOCYTOSIS

51. Show by means of a diagram the difference between endocytosis and exocytosis.

Endocytosis

52. Three types of endocytosis and the substances they move into the cell are:

    a.

    b.

    c.

53. Most endocytotic vesicles fuse with the membranes of _____ wherein the digestive enzymes destroy the contents.

Exocytosis

54. Substances moved out of cells by exocytosis include:

EPITHELIAL TRANSPORT

55. Epithelial cells line _____. The epithelium lining the hollow chamber side is referred to as the _____ membrane, while the membrane on the opposite surface is the _____ membrane.

56. Two ways substances can cross the epithelium are:

    a.

    b.

Glands

57. The function of glands is to secrete substances into:

    a.

    b.

    c.

58. Exocrine glands have secretions that flow through _____ . Examples of exocrine glands include _____ .

59. Endocrine glands are _____ glands whose secretions are released directly into the interstitial space and then into the blood.

60. Hormones are released from (*exocrine, endocrine*) glands.

Review the SUMMARY, REVIEW QUESTIONS, and THOUGHT QUESTIONS at the end of this chapter in your textbook.

CHAPTER 6 ANSWER KEY

1. Diffusion is the movement of molecules from regions of higher concentration to regions of lower concentration by random thermal motion. An example is oxygen.

2. flux

3. a. one-way flux of molecules from an area of higher concentration to an area of lower concentration
   b. one-way flux of molecules from an area of lower concentration to an area of higher concentration
   c. net flux, which is the difference between a and b

4. greater

5. a. I   b. D   c. I

6. $F = k_p A(C_o - C_i)$

7. F = net flux
   k_p = membrane permeability constant
   A = surface area of the membrane
   C_o = concentration of molecules outside the membrane
   C_i = concentration of molecules inside the membrane

8. $C_i > C_o$

9. nonpolar; oxygen, carbon dioxide, fatty acids, steroid hormones

10. See Fig. 6-5, page 122, and Fig. 6-6, page 123.

11. A separation of electric charge exists across the plasma membrane known as the membrane potential, with the inside of the cell negative with respect to the outside. Since ions are charged, there will be an electric force attracting positive ions into the cell and repelling negative ions from coming into the cell. There is also a concentration (chemical) gradient across the membrane for these ions. Therefore the net flux of ions across the membrane depends on both the electrical and chemical gradients across the membrane.

12. channel gating

13. a. receptor-linked channels
    b. voltage-sensitive channels
    c. stretch-activated channels

14. See Fig. 6-8, page 125.

15. 0.2 percent

16. a. the degree of transporter saturation
    b. the number of transport proteins in the membrane
    c. the rate at which conformational change in the transport proteins occurs

17. See Fig. 6-9, page 126.

18. a. facilitated diffusion   b. active transport

19. Facilitated diffusion is the movement of solute from higher to lower concentrations using transport proteins which are not coupled to an energy source, and the transport proteins may become saturated with increasing solute concentrations.

20. See Fig. 6-10, page 127.

21. glucose

22. Active transport is the movement of solute from lower to higher concentrations using transport proteins which are coupled to an energy source, and the transport proteins may become saturated with increasing solute concentrations.

23. metabolism (ATP)

24. a. primary active transport (direct use of ATP)
    b. secondary active transport (use of an ion concentration gradient across the membrane to drive the process)

25. the transport protein

26. a. Na^+, K^+-ATPase   c. H^+-ATPase
    b. Ca^{2+}-ATPase   d. H^+, K^+-ATPase

27. three, out of, two, into

28. an ion concentration gradient

29. solute, an ion (often sodium)

30. downhill, uphill, cotransport, countertransport

31. amino acid

32. calcium

33. Osmosis is the net diffusion of water from a region of higher water concentration to an area of lower water concentration.

34. $1000 \text{ g}/18 = 55.5 \, M$ (wt. of 1 L water/mol wt. of water)

35. decrease

36. a. two   c. three   e. one
    b. three   d. one   f. one

37. osmolarity

38. 1 mol

39. 2, 6

40. See Fig. 6-19, page 135.

41. See Fig. 6-20, page 136.

42. Osmolarity is the number of osmotically active particles per unit volume. Osmotic pressure is pressure that must be applied to a solution to *prevent* net flow of water across the membrane.

43. greater

44. sodium, chloride, potassium, organic solutes

45. 300

46. shrink, hypertonic

47. hypotonic, from outside the cells to inside the cells

48. isotonic

49. An isosmotic solution implies the osmolarity of a solution (300 mOsm) relative to the extracellular fluid (300 mOsm) without regard for whether the solute is penetrating or not. An isotonic solution takes into consideration only the nonpenetrating solute (300 mOsm) in comparison to the extracellular fluid (300 mOsm).

50. isotonic. This will prevent cell shrinking or swelling.

51. See Fig. 6-22, page 139.

52. a. fluid endocytosis: extracellular fluid
    b. absorptive endocytosis: specific molecules
    c. phagocytosis: large particles such as bacteria and debris from damaged tissues

53. lysosomes

54. membrane-impermeable molecules synthesized by cells such as proteins

55. hollow organs or tubes, lumenal, basolateral

56. a. paracellular pathway   b. transcellular pathway

57. a. hollow organs   b. blood   c. skin

58. ducts, sweat and salivary glands

59. ductless

60. endocrine

CHAPTER
7
HOMEOSTATIC MECHANISMS
AND CELLULAR COMMUNICATION

GENERAL CHARACTERISTICS OF HOMEOSTATIC CONTROL SYSTEMS

1. Define homeostasis.

2. Define steady state.

3. Define operating point.

4. Differentiate between negative and positive feedback control systems.

5. A(n) _____ signal must be present to drive a homeostatic control system to maintain a stable internal environment in a biological system.

Review Table 7-1, page 154.

Feedforward Regulation

6. What are the advantages of feedforward regulation?

   a.

   b.

   c.

Acclimatization

7. Acclimatization is an improved ability to respond to _____ with no change in _____ .

8. If acclimatization develops early in life and becomes irreversible, it is known as _____ . An example of this is:

Biological Rhythms

9. A(n) _____ rhythm cycles approximately once every 24 h. Examples include:

10. A(n) _____ rhythm is a rhythm that exists (persists) in the absence of environmental cues.

11. _____ rhythms are environmental time cues that reset the internal clock, such as jet lag or nightshift working.

12. The part of the brain thought to be the "pacemaker" for circadian rhythms is the _____ .

13. Knowledge of circadian rhythms is beneficial in medical treatments. Give an example.

Aging and Homeostasis

14. Describe the effects of aging on the body's cells.

    a.

    b.

15. Two theories for changes in cells associated with aging are:

    a.

    b.

THE BALANCE CONCEPT AND CHEMICAL HOMEOSTASIS

16. Three states of body balance of a chemical and a brief description of each are:

    a. stable balance: loss equals gain

    b.

    c.

COMPONENTS OF HOMEOSTATIC SYSTEMS

Reflexes

17. List the components of a reflex arc.
    a.
    b.
    c.
    d.
    e.

18. The major effectors of biological control systems are _____ and _____.

Review Table 7-3, page 161.

Local Homeostatic Responses

19. Local homeostatic responses are stimulus-response events but occur only in the area of the _____, with neither nerves nor hormones being involved.

20. Using a diagram, show how the following chemical messengers can perform inter-cellular communication:

hormone   neurotransmitter   neurohormone   paracrine   autocrine

21. Differentiate between paracrine and autocrine agents.

Eicosanoids

22. Eicosanoids are produced from _____ in the plasma membrane and include _____ , _____ , _____ , and _____ .

23. The enzyme which, when activated by a stimulus, splits off arachidonic acid from the membrane phospholipids is _____ .

24. Arachidonic acid is split into two pathways in the presence of two different enzymes: _____ and _____ .

25. The products of cyclooxygenase activity are:

26. The products of lipoxygenase activity are:

27. Eicosanoids are categorized as paracrine and autocrine agents. (*true, false*)

28. Aspirin blocks what enzyme in the eicosanoid pathway?

29. Complete the following diagram.

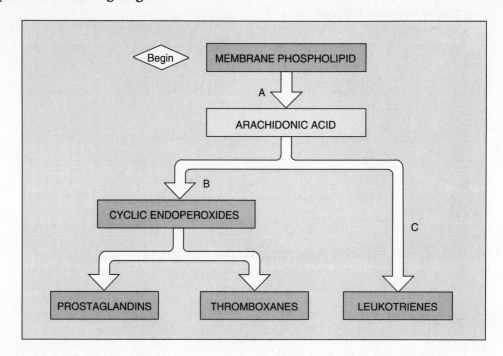

30. The enzymes involved at points A, B, and C are:

A:

B:

C:

RECEPTORS

31. Define a receptor.

32. Match:
    a. specificity
    b. saturation
    c. affinity
    d. competition
    e. antagonist
    f. agonist

    a. ___ a drug that mimics a normal messenger's action
    b. ___ the ability of a receptor to react with only a limited number of messenger molecules
    c. ___ a drug that binds to a receptor but does not elicit a cellular response
    d. ___ the degree to which receptors are bound by messenger molecules
    e. ___ molecules similar in structure, binding with the same receptor
    f. ___ the strength with which a messenger binds to a receptor

Regulation of Receptors

33. In the presence of chronic high levels of a messenger, the receptors will be (*up-*, *down-*) regulated.

SIGNAL TRANSDUCTION MECHANISMS
FOR PLASMA MEMBRANE RECEPTORS

34. The receptors for lipid-soluble messengers are located _____ , while the receptors for lipid-insoluble messengers are located _____ .

35. Diagram the signal transduction mechanism for receptors influencing ion channels.

36. Diagram a G-protein-dependent signal transduction mechanism.

37. Diagram a cyclic-AMP second-messenger signal transduction mechanism.

38. ATP is converted to cAMP by the enzyme _____ , and cAMP is converted to AMP by the enzyme _____ .

39. Intracellular cAMP activates the enzyme _____ , which phosphorylates many different proteins for cellular responses of secretion, contraction, etc.

40. Receptor activation of what membrane protein causes an inhibition of adenylate cyclase and therefore decreases the cAMP in the cell as well as decreases the phosphorylation of key proteins in the cell? _____

Guanylate Cyclase and Cyclic GMP

41. Describe the guanylate cyclase-cGMP system.

Phospholipase C, Diacylglycerol, and Inositol Triphosphate

42. Diagram the signal transduction mechanism by which PIP_2 becomes IP_3 and DAG.

43. The enzyme that converts PIP_2 to IP_3 and DAG is _____.

Ion Channels Controlled by G Proteins

44. Using a diagram, show how ion channels are *directly* controlled by G proteins, where no second messenger is involved.

Calcium as a Second Messenger

45. Receptor activation can lead to an increase in cytosolic calcium levels by:

    a.

    b.

    c.

46. How does increased cytosolic calcium lead to cellular responses?

Review the SUMMARY, REVIEW QUESTIONS, and THOUGHT QUESTIONS at the end of this chapter in your textbook.

CHAPTER 7 ANSWER KEY

1. Homeostasis is the maintenance of a stable internal environment through compensatory homeostatic control mechanisms.

2. A steady-state system is one which has a variable that is not changing but requires energy to be added continuously to keep the variable constant.

3. An operating point is the point of the steady-state variable around which a system operates.

4. In a negative-feedback control system, changes in the variable lead to responses that move the variable in the <u>opposite</u> direction, thus leading to stability in the system. In a positive feedback control system, a change in the variable leads to responses that increase the variable away from the set point even further, <u>not</u> favoring stability.

5. error

6. a. It anticipates changes in a regulated variable.
   b. It increases the speed of a body's homeostatic response.
   c. It minimizes fluctuations in the variable being regulated.

7. environmental stress, genetics (genetic endowment)

8. developmental acclimatization, barrel-chested natives living in the high-altitude Andes Mountains in a low-oxygen environment. This developmental acclimatization increases their gas exchange capabilities.

9. circadian; wake-sleep, body temperature, some hormone concentrations in the blood

10. free-running

11. phase-shift

12. hypothalamus

13. Asthma usually flares up at night. Time-released medication is given so that its maximal release is between midnight and 8 a.m.

14. a. There is a decrease in the number of cells in the body as a result of decreased mitosis and increased cell death.
    b. There is cellular malfunction, especially in the DNA, RNA, and cell proteins.

15. a. There is increased damage to the macromolecules (DNA and RNA).
    b. Cellular senescence is programmed into our genes. (Genes for aging are activated as one gets older.)

16. b. negative balance: loss exceeds gain.
    c. positive balance: gain exceeds loss.

17. a. receptor   c. central integrating center   e. effector
    b. afferent pathway   d. efferent pathway

18. muscles, glands

19. stimulus

20. See Fig. 7-8, page 161.

21. Paracrine agents are agents synthesized and secreted specifically for regulating local cells. They are inactivated by local enzymes and do not enter the bloodstream. Autocrine agents are agents secreted by a cell which then act upon the cell that secreted them.

22. arachidonic acid, prostaglandins, thromboxanes, leukotrienes, prostacyclin

23. phospholipase A_2

24. cyclooxygenase, lipoxygenase

25. prostaglandins, thromboxanes, prostacyclin

26. leukotrienes

27. true

28. cyclooxygenase

29. A: phospholipase A_2 B: cyclooxygenase   C: lipoxygenase

30. A: phospholipase A_2 B: cyclooxygenase   C: lipoxygenase

31. A receptor is a specific protein in either the plasma membrane or in the cytosol with which a chemical mediator combines to exert its effects.

32. a. f   c. e   e. d
    b. a   d. b   f. c

33. down-

34. intracellularly, in the plasma membrane

35. See Fig. 7-12, page 167.

36. See Fig. 7-15, page 169.

37. See Fig. 7-16, page 169.

38. adenylate cyclase, phosphodiesterase

39. cAMP-dependent protein kinase (protein kinase A)

40. G_i

41. Receptor activation of the plasma membrane G protein activates the membrane-bound guanylate cyclase which then generates in the cytosol cGMP. cGMP acts as a second messenger to activate cGMP-dependent protein kinase which phosphorylates proteins to cause cell responses.

42. See Fig. 7-21, page 173.

43. phospholipase C

44. See Fig. 7-22, page 173.

45. a. plasma membrane calcium channels opening
    b. calcium released from the endoplasmic reticulum via IP_3
    c. second messengers inhibiting the active transport of calcium out of the cell

46. Calcium binds with various calcium-binding proteins, most prominently calmodulin, which then activates or inhibits enzymes or other proteins.

CHAPTER
8
NEURAL CONTROL MECHANISMS

Section A. Neural Tissue

1. The two divisions of the nervous system and the components of each are:

   a.

   b.

2. The four parts of a neuron are:
   a.
   b.
   c.
   d.

3. Describe the major function of each of the four parts of a neuron.

   a.

   b.

   c.

   d.

4. Cells in the CNS that lay down myelin are called _____,
   and in the PNS are called _____ .

5. The purpose of myelin is:

6. The part(s) of a neuron that is (are) myelinated is (are): _____ .

7. The movement of materials from the cell body to axon terminals and also from axon terminals to the cell body is known as _____ .

8. Diagram and label in series the three functional types of neurons and indicate which parts are in the CNS and in the PNS.

9. Identify the functional type of neuron:
   a. ___ have no dendrites
   b. ___ cell body and most of the axon extensions are outside the CNS
   c. ___ cell body, dendrites, and axon are inside the CNS
   d. ___ cell body and dendrites are in the CNS, but axons extend outside into the PNS
   e. ___ transmit information into the CNS
   f. ___ transmit information out of the CNS
   g. ___ connect afferent and efferent neurons

10. Define synapse.

11. A neuron that conducts information toward a synapse is a(n) _____ neuron, and a neuron conducting information away from a synapse is a(n) _____ neuron.

12. Draw two neurons interacting with each other. Label the presynaptic and postsynaptic neurons. Indicate the direction of transmission of neural information.

13. The two types of glial cells and their major functions are:

   a.

   b.

NEURAL GROWTH AND REGENERATION

14. The specialized enlargement at the tip of each developing neuron involved in finding the correct route or target for the neuron is called the _____ .

15. Special glycoproteins that aid in neural development are _____ and _____ .

16. PNS neuronal regeneration may occur after injury if the cell body is alive, but CNS neuron regeneration cannot occur. (*true, false*)

Review the SUMMARY and REVIEW QUESTIONS at the end of this section in your textbook.

Section B. Membrane Potentials

17. The formula for Ohm's law is:

18. Insulators have (*high, low*) electrical resistance. Conductors have (*high, low*) electrical resistance. Water has (*high, low*) electrical resistance. Lipid layers of the membrane have (*high, low*) electrical resistance.

THE RESTING MEMBRANE POTENTIAL

19. Define resting membrane potential (RMP).

20. What determines the magnitude of the RMP (e.g., −40 mV, −75 mV, or −100 mV)?

21. What are the major extracellular and intracellular ion concentrations that contribute to the RMP in a resting neuron?

22. Define equilibrium potential.

23. The larger the ion concentration gradient, the (*larger, smaller*) the equilibrium potential.

24. The calculated potassium equilibrium potential for a nerve cell is about _____ mV, while the calculated sodium equilibrium potential is about _____ mV. The resting membrane potential is actually about _____ mV, which is closer to the _____ equilibrium potential because _____ .

25. Since a nerve cell's RMP is not at the equilibrium potential for sodium or potassium, there is a net movement of _____ into the cell and _____ out of the cell.

26. Extracellular sodium and intracellular potassium concentrations are maintained high by _____, which also contribute to the membrane potential because _____ sodium ion(s) is (are) pumped out for every _____ potassium ion(s) pumped into the cell. This type of pump is known as _____ .

GRADED POTENTIALS AND ACTION POTENTIALS

27. Draw on an *X-Y* axis the following events: a resting potential of –70 mV and a depolarization, repolarization, and hyperpolarization event.

Graded Potentials

28. Three important characteristics of graded potentials are:

    a.

    b.

    c.

Action Potentials

Ionic basis of the action potential

29. Draw an action potential (–70 mV to +30 mV). Superimpose on it the permeability changes for sodium (P_{Na}) and potassium (P_K) ions.

30. The depolarization phase of an action potential is due to increased membrane permeability to _____ ions, while the repolarization phase is due to decreased permeability to _____ ions and increased permeability to _____ ions.

31. Very small ionic concentrations move with each action potential, but these ionic gradients are maintained by means of the _____.

Mechanism of ion-channel changes

32. Describe the positive feedback relationship between local current and increased membrane permeability to sodium.

33. What is responsible for inactivation of the voltage-sensitive sodium channels during depolarization?

Threshold

34. Draw a diagram illustrating subthreshold and suprathreshold stimuli and their respective subthresholds and the action potentials generated by these stimuli.

35. Define the all-or-none law.

Refractory periods

36. Differentiate between absolute and relative refractory periods.

37. What molecular events occur during the refractory period?

Action-potential propagation

38. There is a (*direct, inverse*) relationship between fiber diameter and velocity of action-potential propagation.

39. There is a(n) (*direct, inverse*) relationship between myelinated axons and velocity of action-potential propagation.

Review the SUMMARY and REVIEW QUESTIONS at the end of this section in your textbook.

Section C. Synapses

40. Differentiate between convergence and divergence.

41. Whether a postsynaptic cell will fire an action potential or not depends on:

    a.

    b.

FUNCTIONAL ANATOMY OF SYNAPSES

42. Two types of synapses are:

    a.

    b.

43. Diagram a chemical synapse and label the synaptic cleft, synaptic vesicle, terminal of the presynaptic axon, and postsynaptic cell.

44. Discuss how signals are transmitted across the synaptic cleft.

Excitatory Chemical Synapse

45. Differentiate between an EPSP and an IPSP.

ACTIVATION OF THE POSTSYNAPTIC CELL

46. Two EPSPs occurring at different sites on the same cell that summate in the post-synaptic neuron represent (*spatial, temporal*) summation.

47. The part of a neuron with the lowest threshold is the _____ .

SYNAPTIC EFFECTIVENESS

48. List several factors that influence synaptic effectiveness of pre- and postsynaptic events.

NEUROTRANSMITTERS AND NEUROMODULATORS

49. (*Neurotransmitters, neuromodulators*) cause EPSPs and IPSPs, while (*neurotransmitters, neuromodulators*) affect pre- and postsynaptic effects.

50. The actions of neurotransmitters are faster than the actions of neuromodulators. (*true, false*)

Acetylcholine

51. The neurotransmitter acetylcholine (ACh) is synthesized from _____ and _____ and is inactivated by the enzyme _____.

52. Two types of ACh receptors are _____ and _____.

53. Fibers that release ACh are known as _____ fibers.

Biogenic Amines

54. Biogenic amines in the nervous system include _____.

55. Catecholamines include _____.

56. Catecholamine neurotransmitters are broken down by the enzymes _____ and _____.

57. The two types of adrenergic receptors and the second-messenger system each uses are:

    a.

    b.

Serotonin (5-hydroxytryptamine, 5-HT)

58. Major effects of serotonin (neuromodulator) are:

59. LSD (*enhances, inhibits*) serotonin's actions, while some antidepressants (*enhance, inhibit*) serotonin's effects.

Amino Acid Neurotransmitters

60. Examples of excitatory amino acid transmitters are _____; examples of inhibitory amino acid neurotransmitters are _____.

Neuropeptides

61. Neurons that release peptides as neurotransmitters are called _____ neurons.

Review the SUMMARY and REVIEW QUESTIONS at the end of this section in your textbook.

Section D. Structure of the Nervous System

62. A nerve is a group of nerve fibers in the (*CNS, PNS*).

63. A pathway or tract is a group of nerve fibers in the (*CNS, PNS*).

64. A ganglia is a group of cell bodies in the (*CNS, PNS*).

65. Nuclei are a group of cell bodies in the (*CNS, PNS*).

66. The meninges, from outside to in, are the _____ .

CENTRAL NERVOUS SYSTEM: SPINAL CORD

67. Draw a cross-section of the spinal cord indicating gray and white matter, dorsal and ventral roots, spinal nerves, and dorsal root ganglion. Use arrows to indicate the direction of input and output of neural activity.

68. The spinal nerves, which innervate skeletal muscle, are divided into the following levels:

CENTRAL NERVOUS SYSTEM: BRAIN

69. The six subdivisions of the brain are:

70. The forebrain includes the _____ and _____ .

71. The brainstem includes the _____ .

Brainstem

72. The one part of the brain absolutely essential for life is the _____ .

Cerebellum

73. Some major functions of the cerebellum are:

Forebrain

74. The four lobes of the cerebral cortex are:
    a.
    b.
    c.
    d.

75. The bundles of nerve fibers that connect the right and left cerebral hemispheres are called the _____ .

76. Areas within each cerebral hemisphere are connected by _____ fibers.

77. Nuclei that lie deep within the cerebral hemispheres and play an important role in control of movement and posture are the _____ .

Review Table 8-8, page 219, for the functions of the major parts of the brain.

PERIPHERAL NERVOUS SYSTEM

78. There is (are) _____ pair(s) of cranial nerves and _____ pair(s) of spinal nerves.

Peripheral Nervous System: Afferent Division

79. Describe the afferent input in peripheral nerves.

80. The efferent output of the peripheral nervous system is divided into _____ and _____ .

Somatic nervous system

81. The somatic efferent fibers innervate _____ muscle, release _____ as the neurotransmitter, and always lead to muscle _____ .

Autonomic nervous system

82. The autonomic efferent fibers innervate _____ , _____ , and _____ and have ____ neuron(s) between the CNS and the effector organ called the _____ and _____ fibers.

83. The autonomic nervous system is divided into two major divisions: _____ and _____ .

84. Indicate whether the following statements apply to the sympathetic (S) or para-sympathetic (P) division or to both divisions of the ANS.
    a. ____ thoracolumbar outflow
    b. ____ craniosacral outflow
    c. ____ ganglia lie close to the spinal cord
    d. ____ ganglia lie within the organs innervated by the postganglionic neurons
    e. ____ neurotransmitter released between pre- and postganglionic fibers is ACh
    f. ____ neurotransmitter released between postganglionic fiber and effector cell is ACh
    g. ____ neurotransmitter released between postganglionic fiber and effector cell is usually norepinephrine

85. The adrenal medulla, under control of the sympathetic preganglionic fibers, releases primarily _____ (a hormone) into the general circulation.

86. Effector organs which receive dual innervation usually have the sympathetic division exert a (*fight-or-flight, homeostatic*) response, while the parasympathetic division exerts a (*fight-or-flight, homeostatic*) response.

BLOOD SUPPLY, BLOOD-BRAIN BARRIER PHENOMENA, AND CEREBROSPINAL FLUID

87. The nutrient that the brain requires is _____ .

88. Describe the cerebrospinal fluid.

Review the SUMMARY and REVIEW QUESTIONS at the end of this section and the THOUGHT QUESTIONS at the end of this chapter in your textbook.

CHAPTER 8 ANSWER KEY

1. a. central nervous system (CNS)—brain and spinal cord
   b. peripheral nervous system (PNS)—nerves to and from the CNS

2. a. cell body   c. axon
   b. dendrites   d. axon terminals

3. a. cell body: has organelles (nucleus, ribosomes) needed for protein synthesis, receives information from other neurons
   b. dendrites: branched extensions from cell body, receive information from other neurons
   c. axon: single long extension from cell body that transmits signals away from cell body, has initial segment and axon terminals
   d. axon terminals: end of axon branches which release chemical transmitters, may have varicosities

4. oligodendroglia, Schwann cells

5. to increase the speed of electrical transmission along the axons

6. axons

7. axon transport

8. See Fig. 8-4, page 183.

9. a. afferent   d. efferent   f. efferent
   b. afferent   e. afferent   g. interneurons
   c. interneurons

10. A synapse is an anatomical junction between two neurons where one neuron may alter the activity of the other.

11. presynaptic, postsynaptic

12. See Fig. 8-5, page 184.

13. a. oligodendroglia (form myelin)
    b. astroglia (regulate extracellular fluid composition in the CNS, sustain metabolic functions of neurons, influence neurons during development, may take part in information transmission)

14. growth cone

15. cell adhesion molecules (CAMs); nerve growth factor

16. true

17. $I = E/R$, where I = current, E = voltage (electric potential differences), R = resistance

18. high, low, low, high

19. RMP is the potential difference across the membrane with the inside of the cell negative to the outside. By convention, the voltage outside the cell is set at 0 mV.

20. a. ionic concentration differences across the membrane
    b. membrane permeability to the various ions

21. Extracellular (mmol/L): Na^+ = 150, K^+ = 5, Cl^- = 110
    Intracellular (mmol/L): Na^+ = 15, K^+ = 150, Cl^- = 10

22. Equilibrium potential is the membrane potential at which the ion flux due to the ion concentration gradient is equal but opposite to the flux due to the electrical gradient, resulting in *no* net movement of ions.

23. larger

24. −90, +60, −70, potassium; at rest, the membrane is much more permeable to potassium than to sodium

25. sodium, potassium

26. Na, K-ATPase pumps; three; two; electrogenic

27. See Fig. 8-13, page 191.

28. a. They are local potentials.
    b. Their magnitude can be graded.
    c. They die out with distance (within 1 to 2 mm of the site of origin).

29. See Fig. 8-17, page 194.

30. sodium, sodium, potassium

31. Na, K-ATPase pump

32. Depolarization (local current) opens sodium channels which leads to increased sodium permeability which leads to increased sodium moving into the cells which decreases the membrane potential toward the sodium equilibrium potential which leads to opening of more voltage-sensitive channels, etc.

33. a change in sodium channel protein configuration

34. See Fig. 8-19, page 197.

35. Action potentials occur maximally or not at all; i.e., action potentials cannot be graded.

36. During the absolute refractory period, an action potential cannot be elicited no matter how great the stimulus strength. During the relative refractory period, an action potential may be elicited if the stimulus is much greater than threshold.

37. The proteins of the voltage-sensitive ion channels are being restored to their original configuration.

38. direct

39. direct

40. Convergence is neural input from many neurons onto a single neuron, while divergence is the output from one neuron onto many other neurons.

41. a. the number of synapses of presynaptic with postsynaptic sites
    b. the number of excitatory versus inhibitory synapses

42. a. electrical
    b. chemical

43. See Fig. 8-24, page 201.

44. When the action potential reaches the axon terminal, voltage-sensitive calcium channels in the presynaptic terminal open and calcium moves into the terminal from the extracellular fluid. The calcium causes the synaptic vesicles to fuse with the presynaptic membrane and liberate the vesicle neurotransmitter. The neurotransmitter moves across the synaptic cleft and binds to postsynaptic membrane receptors, whereby receptor-operated channels are opened, which causes ion channels to open.

45. An EPSP is a graded (depolarizing) postsynaptic potential which results from neurotransmitter-activated postsynaptic receptors causing increased permeability to sodium, potassium, and other small cations, which brings the membrane potential closer to threshold. An IPSP is a graded (hyperpolarizing) postsynaptic potential which results from neurotransmitter-activated postsynaptic receptors causing increased permeability to chloride and sometimes potassium ions, which moves the membrane potential away from threshold—hyperpolarization.

46. spatial

47. initial segment

48. Presynaptic factors: availability of neurotransmitters, axon terminal membrane potential, axon terminal residual calcium, activation of membrane receptors on presynaptic terminal, certain drugs and diseases
    Postsynaptic factors: immediate past history of electrical state of postsynaptic membrane (i.e., facilitation or inhibition from temporal or spatial summation), effects of other neurotransmitters or neuromodulators acting on postsynaptic neuron; certain drugs and diseases
    (See Table 8-5, page 206.)

49. neurotransmitters; neuromodulators

50. true

51. choline, acetyl coenzyme A, acetylcholinesterase

52. nicotinic, muscarinic

53. cholinergic

54. dopamine, norepinephrine, serotonin, and histamine

55. dopamine, norepinephrine, and epinephrine

56. monoamine oxidase, catechol-O-methyltransferase

57. a. alpha, phospholipase C
    b. beta, cAMP

58. excitatory effects on pathways involved in muscle control and inhibitory effects on pathways mediating sensations and mood control.

59. inhibits, enhance

60. glutamate and aspartate, GABA and glycine

61. peptidergic

62. PNS

63. CNS

64. PNS

65. CNS

66. dura mater, arachnoid, and pia mater

67. See Fig. 8-35, page 215.

68. cervical, thoracic, lumbar, sacral, and coccygeal

69. cerebrum, diencephalon, midbrain, pons, medulla oblongata, and cerebellum

70. cerebrum and diencephalon

71. midbrain, pons, and medulla

72. reticular formation

73. control of skeletal-muscle function as regards coordinating and learning movements, controlling posture and balance

74. frontal, parietal, occipital, temporal

75. corpus callosum

76. association

77. basal ganglia

78. 12, 31

79. The afferent input is primarily from sensory receptors sending information to the CNS. The cell bodies are located in the dorsal root ganglia.

80. somatic, autonomic

81. skeletal, ACh, contraction or excitation

82. smooth muscle, cardiac muscle, glands, two, preganglionic, postganglionic

83. sympathetic, parasympathetic

84. a. S   d. P   f. P
    b. P   e. S and P   g. S
    c. S

85. epinephrine

86. fight or flight, homeostatic

87. glucose

88. Cerebrospinal fluid is a clear fluid, continuously made by the choroid plexus in the ventricles, and surrounds the brain and spinal cord. It fills the cerebral ventricles and subarachnoid space and protects the brain and spinal cord from damage or injury.

CHAPTER
9
THE SENSORY SYSTEMS

1. The three major components in sensory input include:

   a.

   b.

   c.

2. Differentiate between sensation and perception.

RECEPTORS

3. The energy form that activates a receptor is called a(n) _____.

4. The process by which a stimulus is transformed into an electrical response is called _____.

5. The type of energy to which a receptor responds in normal functioning is called its _____.

6. All receptors can be activated by several energy forms if the intensity is high enough. (*true, false*)

7. Define the doctrine of specific nerve energies.

The Receptor Potential

8. List the characteristics of a receptor potential.

9. The magnitude of the graded receptor potential determines the action-potential frequency. (*true, false*)

10. The magnitude of the graded receptor potential determines the magnitude of the action potential. (*true, false*)

11. A major factor that limits action-potential frequency is _____

NEURAL PATHWAYS IN SENSORY SYSTEMS

12. A sensory unit consists of _____.

13. Diagram an example of a receptive field.

Ascending Pathways

14. Differentiate between specific and nonspecific ascending pathways.

15. Diagram an example of specific and nonspecific ascending pathways.

16. Neurons in a *nonspecific* pathway that responds to input from several afferent neurons each activated by a different stimuli (skin pressure, heating, cooling) are called _____ neurons.

17. *Specific* ascending pathways pass to the _____ ,
    except for _____ pathways, and the final neurons terminate on different (specific)
    areas of the _____ .

18. *Nonspecific* pathways pass through the nondiscriminative areas of the _____ ,
    and the final neurons terminate on the _____ .

19. Somatic receptor send afferent information to the _____ cortex located in the
    _____ lobe.

20. Visual receptors send afferent information to the _____cortex located in
    the _____ lobe.

21. Auditory receptors send afferent information to the _____ cortex located in the
    _____ lobe.

ASSOCIATION CORTEX AND PERCEPTUAL PROCESSING

22. Brain areas that lie outside the primary cortical sensory or motor areas but are con-
    nected to them are called _____ .

23. The major function of association areas is:

Factors That Distort Perception

24. List some factors that may distort or alter perception.

25. Three processes required for sensory perception to occur are:

    a.

    b.

    c.

PRIMARY SENSORY CODING

26. The three aspects of a stimulus that are coded are:

 a.

 b.

 c.

27. Several stimulus types or modalities are:

28. All the receptors of an afferent neuron are preferentially sensitive to the same type of stimulus. (*true, false*)

Stimulus Intensity

29. An increase in stimulus intensity is coded by:

 a.

 b.

 c.

Stimulus Location

30. Stimulus location depends on the

 a.

 b.

Lateral inhibition

31. Diagram an example of lateral inhibition that demonstrates how sensory acuity is increased.

Stimulus Duration

32. Diagram the difference between rapidly adapting and slowly adapting receptors. On the top line indicate stimulus application time. On the bottom line indicate action-potential firing of the afferent nerve fiber from the receptor.

33. Give an example of rapidly adapting and slowly adapting receptors in your body.

SOMATIC SENSATION

34. Somatic sensations include:

35. Each somatic sensation has a specific receptor type. (*true, false*)

36. Describe the pathway of the somatosensory input from receptors to the cortex.

37. Roughly diagram the somatosensory cortex showing the areas of the body that have the greatest representation (are most densely innervated).

Touch-Pressure

38. Skin mechanoreceptors that give rise to sensations of touch, movement, and vibration are (*fast, slow*) adapting, while the sensation of pressure comes from receptors that are (*fast, slow*) adapting.

Sense of Posture and Movement

39. The main receptors responsible for the sense of posture and movement are _____, supported by input from _____ and _____.

Pain

40. Receptors that give rise to the sensation of pain are known as _____.

41. The afferent neurons carrying pain into the CNS release the neurotransmitter _____.

42. Referred pain often occurs because both visceral and somatic afferents often converge on the same interneurons in the pain pathway. (*true, false*)

VISION

The Optics of Vision

43. Draw a diagram of the human eye. Include the cornea, lens, pupil, aqueous and vitreous humor, retina, fovea centralis, and optic nerve.

44. Define accommodation.

45. The _____ muscle changes the shape of the lens.

46. Describe how the eye "sees" near objects.

47. Match:

   a. stiffness of the lens
   b. cloudiness of the lens
   c. nearsighted

   d. farsighted
   e. irregular curvature of the lens
   f. increased intraocular pressure

   a. ___ astigmatism
   b. ___ cataract
   c. ___ glaucoma
   d. ___ hyperopia
   e. ___ myopia
   f. ___ presbyopia

48. The anterior chamber of the eye contains the fluid known as _____, while the posterior chamber contains _____.

49. The amount of light entering the eye is controlled by the circular smooth muscle called the _____, which regulates the opening called the _____.

50. Sympathetic stimulation causes the ciliary muscle to (*contract, relax*) and the pupil to (*constrict, dilate*), while parasympathetic stimulation causes the ciliary muscle to (*contract, relax*) and the pupil to (*constrict, dilate*).

Receptor Cells

51. The photoreceptors that respond to very low levels of illumination are _____, and the photoreceptors that respond to brighter light are _____.

52. The photopigments are made up of a protein, _____, and a chromophore, _____.

53. The second messenger involved in photopigment activation is _____, which (*depolarizes, hyperpolarizes*) the photoreceptors and (*increases, decreases*) neurotransmitter release.

Neural Pathways of Vision

54. Diagram the visual pathway from the rods and cones to the cerebral cortex.

55. Half of the optic nerves cross to the opposite side of the brain in the _____.

56. The cones contain these color-sensitive photopigments: _____, _____, _____.

Eye Movement

57. Eye movement is regulated by six (*skeletal, cardiac, smooth*) muscles.

HEARING

Sound

58. Sound wave amplitude determines _____, and sound wave frequency determines _____.

59. Describe the sequence of sound transmission.

60. Draw a diagram of the cochlea, labeling the scala vestibuli, scala tympani, cochlear duct, helicotrema, oval window, and round window.

61. The scala vestibuli opens into the scala tympani at the distal end of the cochlear duct at a structure called the _____.

62. Diagram a cross section of the organ of Corti.

Hair Cells of the Organ of Corti

63. Movement of the basilar membrane causes the stereocilia to come in contact with the _____ membrane, causing ion channels to open and receptor potentials to be generated, leading to action potentials.

VESTIBULAR SYSTEM

64. The vestibular apparatus lies in the temporal bone and consists of three _____ and two saclike swellings, the _____ and _____.

The Semicircular Canals

65. The semicircular canals detect (*angular, linear*) acceleration, while the utricle and saccule respond to (*angular, linear*) acceleration.

CHEMICAL SENSES

Taste

66. Taste receptors are called _____ and are specialized into sensing four basic groups of taste: _____, _____, _____, _____.

67. The _____ lobe of the brain is the CNS center for afferent fibers from the taste receptor cells.

Smell

68. The receptors for the sense of smell (specialized afferent neurons) are found in the _____.

Review the SUMMARY, REVIEW QUESTIONS, and THOUGHT QUESTIONS at the end of this chapter in your textbook.

CHAPTER 9 ANSWER KEY

1. a. sensory receptors
   b. neural pathway from the receptors to the brain
   c. the parts of the brain that deal primarily with processing of sensory information

2. Sensation results from sensory information reaching consciousness, while perception is the understanding of the sensation's meaning.

3. stimulus

4. transduction

5. adequate stimulus

6. true

7. This doctrine states that for every kind of sensation there is a special type of receptor whose activation always gives rise to that sensation.

8. A receptor potential results from the opening or closing of ion channels in a specialized receptor membrane; this receptor potential is graded; it may cause the release of a neurotransmitter if the receptor membrane is on another cell; the magnitude of the receptor potential decreases with distance from its origin; if of sufficient magnitude to reach threshold, an action potential is elicited.

9. true

10. false

11. threshold

12. a single afferent neuron with all its receptor endings

13. See Fig. 9-4, page 236.

14. Specific ascending pathways convey information about a single type of stimuli. Non-specific pathways carry information from several different types of receptors and convey general information.

15. See Fig. 9-7, page 238.

16. polymodal

17. brainstem and thalamus, olfactory, cerebral cortex

18. brainstem and thalamus, nonspecific areas of the cerebral cortex

19. somatosensory, parietal

20. visual, occipital

21. auditory, temporal

22. cortical association areas

23. the complex analysis of incoming information

24. adaptation of the sensory information along afferent pathways; emotions, personality, experience; subconscious damping of some sensory information; damaged neural pathways; drugs; illusions

25. a. transduction of the sensory stimulus to a receptor potential and action potential
    b. transmission of the action potentials through the appropriate ascending pathways
    c. analysis of incoming information in the appropriate lobes and association areas

26. a. stimulus type
    b. intensity
    c. location

27. heat, cold, sound, pressure

28. true

29. a. an increase in frequency of action potential firing
    b. an increase in recruitment of "neighboring" afferent neurons (or spatial summation)

30. a. size of the receptive field covered by an afferent neuron
    b. overlap of nearby receptive fields

31. See Fig. 9-15, page 243.

32. See Fig. 9-16, page 244.

33. Rapidly adapting receptors are found on our skin and result in the rapid fading of the sensation of our clothes pressing on our skin. Slowly adapting receptors help maintain our upright posture (from muscle and joint receptors).

34. touch-pressure, posture and movement, temperature and pain

35. true

36. Afferent input from somatic receptors enters the spinal cord and synapses with neurons that form the specific ascending pathways, passing through the brainstem and thalamus and ending in a specific area of the somatosensory cortex. Crossing over or decussation occurs in the spinal cord or brainstem. Sensory information from the left side of the body goes to the right somatosensory cortex, and vice versa.

37. See Fig. 9-20, page 247.

38. fast, slow

39. muscle-spindle stretch receptors, vision, the vestibular apparatus of the ear

40. nociceptors

41. substance P

42. true

43. See Fig. 9-23, page 250.

44. Accommodation is the change in lens shape to focus the image on the fovea of the retina.

45. ciliary

46. The ciliary (circular) muscle contracts, tension is released on the lens via the zonular fibers, and the lens bulges to bend the light rays to image them properly on the retina.

47. a. e   c. f   e. c
    b. b   d. d   f. a

48. aqueous humor, vitreous humor

49. iris, pupil

50. relax, dilate, contract, constrict

51. rods, cones

52. opsin, retinal

53. cyclic GMP, hyperpolarizes, decreases

54. See Fig. 9-31, page 255.

55. optic chiasm

56. red, green, blue

57. skeletal

58. loudness, pitch

59. a. Sound waves enter the outer ear and press against the tympanic membrane (air conduction).
    b. This causes movement of the malleus, incus, and stapes against the oval window in the middle ear (bone conduction).

c. Movement of the oval window sets up pressure waves in the fluid-filled cochlea (fluid conduction).

60. See Fig. 9-37, page 260.

61. helicotrema

62. See Fig. 9-40, page 262.

63. tectorial

64. semicircular ducts (canals), utricle, saccule

65. angular, linear

66. taste buds; sweet, sour, salty, bitter

67. parietal

68. olfactory mucosa (upper part of the nasal cavity)

CHAPTER
10
HORMONAL CONTROL MECHANISMS

HORMONE STRUCTURES AND SYNTHESIS

1. The three chemical classes of hormones are:

   a.

   b.

   c.

2. Examples of amine hormones are:

   a.

   b.

   c.

   d.

Thyroid hormones

3. Thyroid hormones include _____ , _____ , and _____ .

4. T_4 and T_3 contain the amino acid _____ and atoms of _____ .
   These hormones are stored in the thyroid cells bound to the protein _____ .

5. The biologically active thyroid hormone is _____ .

6. Draw the chemical structures for T_4 and T_3.

Adrenal medullary hormones and dopamine

7. Catecholamines include the amines _____, _____, and _____ .

Peptide Hormones

8. Differentiate among preprohormone, prohormone, and hormone.

Steroid Hormones

9. The precursor molecule for all steroid hormones is _____ .

10. Steroid hormones are produced by the following organs:

    a.

    b.

    c.

Hormones of the adrenal cortex

11. Name the hormones released from the adrenal cortex that are classified as:

    a. Mineralocorticoids:

    b. Glucocorticoids:

    c. Androgens:

12. Mineralocorticoids exert effects on:

13. Glucocorticoids exert effects on:

14. Adrenal androgens exert effects on:

15. The three zones of the adrenal cortex (from outer to inner) and the hormones each zone secretes are:

    a.

    b.

    c.

Hormones of the gonads

16. The primary sex hormone released from the testes is _____, while the primary sex hormones released from the ovaries are _____ and _____ .

HORMONE TRANSPORT IN THE BLOOD

17. Fill in the blanks:

	Carried in plasma	Location of receptors
Peptides and catecholamines	a. _____	c. _____
Steroids and thyroid hormones	b. _____	d. _____

18. The biologically active form of a hormone is the (*free, bound*) hormone.

HORMONE METABOLISM AND EXCRETION

19. The body organs that play a major role in the metabolism and excretion of hormones are the _____ and the _____.

20. An example of a hormone that is converted into its active form *after* it is secreted into the bloodstream to act on its target cells is:

MECHANISMS OF HORMONE ACTION

Hormone Receptors

21. Up-regulation of receptors, an increase in the number of receptors, occurs in response to prolonged (*low, high*) concentrations of a hormone.

22. Permissiveness, a form of hormone-hormone interaction, means:

Events Elicited by Hormone-Receptor Binding

23. Using a diagram show how steroid and thyroid hormones enter target cells, bind to their receptors, and effect protein synthesis.

24. Normal circulating levels of hormones exert (*physiological, pharmacological*) effects, while large doses of hormones usually given for therapeutic reasons exert (*physiological, pharmacological*) effects.

TYPES OF INPUTS THAT CONTROL HORMONE SECRETION

25. Types of inputs that act directly on endocrine glands to stimulate or inhibit hormone secretion are:

   a.

   b.

   c.

   d.

26. Diagram the negative-feedback loop for plasma glucose regulation by insulin.

27. Diagram several pathways by which the nervous system influences hormone secretion.

28. A hormone that stimulates the secretion of another hormone is known as a _____ hormone.

CONTROL SYSTEMS INVOLVING THE HYPOTHALAMUS AND PITUITARY

29. The two lobes of the pituitary gland are:

    a.

    b.

30. The anterior pituitary has a (*glandular, neural*) connection with the hypothalamus, whereas the posterior pituitary has a (*glandular, neural*) connection with the hypothalamus.

31. The hypothalamic-pituitary portal vessels carry blood between the hypothalamus and the _____ . The short portal vessels carry blood from the _____ to the _____ .

Posterior Pituitary Hormones

32. The two major posterior pituitary hormones are _____ and _____ . These hormones are synthesized in the _____ and stored in the _____ . The target organs for these hormones are the

    _____ .

33. Two other hormones recently associated with the posterior pituitary are _____ . These hormones help control the release of prolactin from the _____ and use the _____ portal vessels in doing so.

The Hypothalamus and Anterior Pituitary

34. Hormones produced by the hypothalamus are collectively called _____ hormones.

35. List the hypothalamic and anterior pituitary hormones and their specific target organs.

36. Two hypophysiotropic hormones that inhibit rather than release anterior pituitary hormones are _____ and _____ .

37. A single hormone is often produced at multiple sites. (*true, false*)

38. A hypophysiotropic hormone can cause secretion of more than one anterior pituitary hormone. (*true, false*)

39. All the hypophysiotropic hormones are _____ except for _____,
which is a(n) _____.

40. Hypophysiotropic hormones also appear in places other than the hypothalamus and
act as _____.

Neural control of hypophysiotropic hormones

41. Higher CNS input influences hypophysiotropic hormonal output. Using a diagram
show how stress or neural input from other brain areas influences the hypothalamic–
pituitary–target organ axis for CRH–ACTH–cortisol output. Include the negative-
feedback control.

Hormonal feedback control of the hypothalamus and anterior pituitary

42. Differentiate between a long-loop and short-loop negative feedback. Give an example
of each.

TYPES OF ENDOCRINE DISORDERS

43. Three categories of endocrine disorders are:

a.

b.

c.

44. Differentiate between primary and secondary endocrine disorders.

45. If there is a *primary hyposecretion* disorder of the thyroid gland itself, will the following be increased (I) or decreased (D)?

    a. ___ plasma thyroid hormone levels

    b. ___ circulating levels of TSH

46. If there is a *secondary hyposecretion* disorder of the thyroid, will the following be increased (I) or decreased (D)?

    a. ___ plasma thyroid hormone levels

    b. ___ circulating levels of TSH

47. If there is a *primary hypersecretion* disorder of the thyroid gland itself, will the following be increased (I) or decreased (D)?

    a. ___ plasma thyroid hormone levels

    b. ___ circulating levels of TSH

48. If there is a *secondary hypersecretion* disorder of the thyroid, will the following be increased (I) or decreased (D)?

    a. ___ plasma thyroid hormone levels

    b. ___ circulating levels of TSH

49. What are some factors that contribute to hyporesponsiveness to normal circulating levels of hormones?

Review the SUMMARY and REVIEW QUESTIONS at the end of this chapter in your textbook.

CHAPTER 10 ANSWER KEY

1. a. amines   b. peptides   c. steroids

2. a. thyroid hormones   b. epinephrine   c. norepinephrine   d. dopamine

3. thyroxine, triiodothyronine, calcitonin

4. tyrosine, iodine, thyroglobulin

5. triiodothyronine

6. See Fig. 10-1, page 277.

7. epinephrine, norepinephrine, dopamine

8. Preprohormones are initially synthesized by the ribosomes which are modified (cleaved) into prohormones by enzymes in the endoplasmic reticulum. The prohormones are packaged in the secretory vesicles and cleaved to yield the active hormones.

9. cholesterol

10. a. gonads   b. adrenal cortex   c. placenta

11. a. aldosterone
    b. cortisol, corticosterone
    c. dehydroepiandrosterone, androstenedione

12. salt metabolism

13. glucose and other organic nutrient metabolism

14. masculinization

15. a. zona glomerulosa (aldosterone)
    b. zona fasciculata (primarily cortisol with some androgens)
    c. zona reticularis (primarily androgens with some cortisol)

16. testosterone, estrogen, progesterone

17. a. free   c. plasma membrane
    b. bound to a carrier protein   d. cytosol and/or nucleus

18. free

19. liver, kidneys

20. thyroxine to triiodothyronine, testosterone to dihydrotestosterone

21. low

22. hormone A must be present for the full effectiveness of hormone B's effect

23. See Fig. 10-8, page 283.

24. physiological, pharmacological

25. a. plasma ion concentrations   c. neurotransmitters
    b. plasma organic nutrient concentrations   d. other hormones

26. See Fig. 10-11, page 285.

27. See Fig. 10-12, page 285.

28. trophic

29. a. anterior pituitary (adenohypophysis)
    b. posterior pituitary (neurohypophysis)

30. glandular, neural

31. anterior pituitary, posterior pituitary, anterior pituitary

32. oxytocin, vasopressin (ADH), hypothalamus (in specific nuclei), posterior pituitary neurons; kidneys (vasopressin), breasts and uterus (oxytocin)

33. dopamine and prolactin releasing factor (PRF), anterior pituitary, short

34. hypophysiotropic

35. See Fig. 10-19, page 293.

36. somatostatin, dopamine (prolactin inhibiting hormone)

37. true

38. true

39. peptides, dopamine, amine

40. neurotransmitters or neuromodulators

41. See Fig. 10-20, page 294.

42. Long-loop feedback exerts its effects by means of the target organ hormone feeding back to the hypothalamus and/or anterior pituitary. Examples include TRH-TSH-thyroid hormone and CRH-ACTH-cortisol. Short-loop feedback exerts its effect by means of the anterior pituitary hormone feeding back to the hypothalamus. Examples include prolactin and growth hormone. See Fig. 10-22, page 296.

43. a. hyposecretion   b. hypersecretion   c. hyporesponsiveness

44. Primary disorders are those in which the defect is in the cells that secrete the hormone. Secondary disorders are those in which there is too little or too much of the tropic hormone (from the anterior pituitary).

45. a. D   b. I

46. a. D   b. D

47. a. I   b. D

48. a. I   b. I

49. a lack of or deficiency in the receptors for the hormone, a defect in the coupling of the receptor to the signal transduction mechanism, a lack of specific enzymes necessary to activate the secreted hormone into its biologically active form

CHAPTER

11

MUSCLE

Section A. Skeletal Muscle

1. The three types of muscle are:
   a.
   b.
   c.

STRUCTURE

2. What is the relationship between a muscle and a muscle fiber?

3. Muscle is attached to bone by means of _____ .

4. Skeletal muscle is (*striated, smooth*) and (*multinucleated, mononucleated*).

5. Myofibrils are composed of thick filaments known as _____ and thin filaments known as _____ .

6. Draw a sarcomere. Include the Z lines, A band, I band, actin, myosin, M line, and H zone.

7. In a cross section through the A band, every myosin is surrounded by _____ actins and every actin is surrounded by _____ myosins.

8. The force-generating structures of muscle cells are the _____, which are part of the myosin molecule.

MOLECULAR MECHANISMS OF CONTRACTION

9. Define contraction as it is used in muscle physiology.

Sliding-Filament Mechanism

10. Describe the sliding-filament mechanism of muscle contraction.

11. The four steps that occur during the cross-bridge cycle are:

    a.

    b.

    c.

    d.

12. The two major functions that ATP plays in cross-bridge activity are:

    a.

    b.

13. ATP is required for muscle (*contraction, relaxation*) because it is essential for the (*association, dissociation*) of actin and myosin. After death, in the absence of ATP, the condition known as _____ occurs.

Role of Calcium, Troponin, and Tropomyosin in Contraction

14. Diagram the relationship of actin, troponin, and tropomyosin.

15. Tropomyosin has a length approximately equal to _____ actin molecule(s).

16. _____ blocks the myosin binding sites on the actin molecule, preventing cross-bridge formation.

17. _____ binds to troponin, which alters the tropomyosin to expose the myosin binding sites on the actin molecule.

Excitation-Contraction Coupling

18. Describe the steps involved in excitation-contraction coupling which leads to muscle contraction and relaxation.

19. The action potential travels from the muscle-cell membrane to the sarcoplasmic reticulum via the _____.

20. The calcium storage areas (enlarged areas of the sarcoplasmic reticulum) in muscle cells are known as _____.

21. _____ provides the energy to resequester calcium back into the lateral sacs for muscle relaxation to occur.

22. The three functions of ATP in muscle contraction are:

    a.

    b.

    c.

Membrane Excitation: The Neuromuscular Junction

23. Motor neurons (somatic efferent neurons) are neurons that innervate _____ .

24. A motor unit includes:

25. The motor end plate is:

26. The neuromuscular junction is:

27. The action potential in the axon terminal of a motor neuron depolarizes the nerve membrane and causes _____ channels to open, which allows _____ to diffuse into the axon terminal. This causes release of the neurotransmitter _____ .

28. When acetylcholine binds to the motor end plate, a(n) _____ potential is generated when _____ and _____ ion channels are opened.

29. Diagram the events at the neuromuscular junction that lead to an action potential in a muscle fiber.

30. Every action potential in a motor neuron elicits an action potential in each muscle fiber in its motor unit. (*true, false*)

31. Neuromuscular junctions in skeletal muscle may be excitatory or inhibitory. (*true, false*)

32. The enzyme that breaks down acetylcholine is _____ and is located in the _____.

Review Table 11-2, page 319, for a summary of the sequence of events that lead from an action potential in a motor neuron to the contraction and relaxation of a skeletal-muscle fiber.

33. Three mechanisms by which neuromuscular transmission may be blocked are:

    a.

    b.

    c.

MECHANICS OF SINGLE-FIBER CONTRACTION

34. Differentiate between muscle tension and load.

35. Differentiate among isometric, isotonic, and lengthening contractions.

36. During the recording of isometric contraction, _____ is measured. During the recording of isotonic contraction, _____ is measured.

Twitch Contractions

37. Draw an (a) isometric and (b) isotonic twitch. Be sure to label the X and Y axes. Indicate the time of the electrical event (action potential). Label the latent period and contraction time.

38. Fill in the blanks:

   a. isometric twitch   b. isotonic twitch

   a. ___ has longer latent period

   b. ___ has longer duration of contraction

   c. ___ is influenced by magnitude of the load lifted

Frequency-Tension Relation

39. An increased frequency of firing of action potentials leads to increased muscle tension generation. This is known as _____ . A sustained muscle contraction in response to repetitive action potentials is known as _____ .

40. The tension generated by a single twitch is (*greater than, equal to, less than*) the tension generated by a sustained contraction.

Length-Tension Relation

41. Draw a length-tension curve for a muscle fiber. Indicate the optimal length (l_0).

42. Why is the greatest tension generated at l_0?

Load-Velocity Relation

43. The velocity of muscle-fiber shortening (*increases, decreases*) with increasing loads.

SKELETAL-MUSCLE ENERGY METABOLISM

44. Three sources of ATP for muscle contraction are:

   a.

   b.

   c.

45. The sources of muscle glucose for glycolysis are:

    a.

    b.

Muscle Fatigue

46. Some of the factors that contribute to skeletal-muscle fatigue are:

47. Central command fatigue is:

TYPES OF SKELETAL MUSCLE FIBERS

48. Slow-oxidative fibers have (*high, low*) myosin-ATPase activity with (*high, low*) oxidative capacity.

49. Fast-oxidative fibers have (*high, low*) myosin-ATPase activity with (*high, low*) oxidative capacity.

50. Fast-glycolytic fibers have (*high, low*) myosin-ATPase activity with (*high, low*) oxidative capacity.

51. Glycolytic fibers usually have (*larger, smaller*) diameters than oxidative fibers.

52. The fiber type that fatigues rapidly is _____ , while the fiber type that is resistant to fatigue is _____ .

Review Table 11-3, page 328.

WHOLE-MUSCLE CONTRACTION

53. A whole muscle is made up of many _____ organized into _____ , and all muscle fibers in a single motor unit are of the same type.

54. Most muscles are composed of _____ fiber types.

55. Muscles which need to maintain their activity for long periods of time without fatigue (postural support muscles) contain a large proportion of _____ fibers.

56. Muscles that produce large amounts of tension over a short period of time (weight lifting) contain a large proportion of _____ fibers.

Control of Muscle Tension

57. The total tension a muscle develops depends on

    a.

    b.

58. The number of fibers contracting at any time depends on

    a.

    b.

59. The number of fibers in a motor unit in muscles of the eye are (*fewer, greater*) than the number of fibers in a motor unit in postural muscles.

60. (*Fine, gross*) control of muscle tension is possible in muscles with small motor units.

61. A motor unit of 100 fast-glycolytic fibers produces (*more, less*) force than a motor unit composed of 100 slow-oxidative fibers.

62. Increasing the number of motor units that are active in a muscle is called _____, which is controlled by the higher centers of the brain.

Muscle Adaptation to Exercise

63. Differentiate between muscle atrophy and hypertrophy.

64. During muscle hypertrophy, muscle fiber numbers (*increase, decrease, do not change*).

65. Exercise of low intensity and long duration (swimming, jogging—"aerobic") affects the _____ fibers by increasing the number of mitochondria as well as increasing the number of capillaries around these fibers.

66. Exercise of short duration and high-intensity (weight lifting—"strength training") affects the _____ fibers by increasing the synthesis of actin and myosin and therefore increasing fiber diameter and glycolytic enzymes.

67. Muscle soreness after excessive exercise is a result of:

Lever Action of Muscles and Bones

68. (*Flexion, extension*) refers to a decrease in the angle at a joint, and (*flexion, extension*) refers to an increase in the angle at a joint.

69. For forearm flexion to occur, the (*biceps, triceps*) muscle is the agonist, while the (*biceps, triceps*) muscle is the antagonist.

70. All muscles exert only a pulling force. (*true, false*)

Skeletal-Muscle Disease

71. Match:

    a. hypocalcemic tetany
    b. muscular dystrophy
    c. myasthenia gravis
    d. polio

    a. ___ viral disease that destroys motor neurons

    b. ___ involuntary tetanic muscle contractions due to decreased extracellular calcium

    c. ___ genetic disease characterized by progressive degeneration of skeletal and cardiac muscle

    d. ___ muscle disease characterized by a decrease in the number of acetylcholine receptors

Review the SUMMARY and REVIEW QUESTIONS at the end of this section in your textbook.

Section B. Smooth Muscle

STRUCTURE

72. Smooth muscle is innervated by:

73. The diameter of a smooth-muscle cell is (*greater than, equal to, less than*) the diameter of a skeletal-muscle cell.

74. Describe the arrangement of the thick and thin filaments in a smooth-muscle cell.

75. Smooth muscle has about _____ the myosin concentration as skeletal muscle and about _____ the actin concentration as skeletal muscle.

76. Smooth-muscle contraction occurs by the sliding-filament mechanism, similar to skeletal-muscle contraction, and also exhibits a length-tension relationship. (*true, false*)

CONTRACTION AND ITS CONTROL

Cross-Bridge Activation

77. Diagram the events that occur in smooth and skeletal muscle when cytosolic calcium increases which leads to cross-bridge cycling and tension generation.

78. The calcium-binding protein present in smooth-muscle cells that is related to troponin in skeletal-muscle cells is _____.

79. The enzyme _____ uses ATP to phosphorylate myosin cross bridges, which bind to actin filaments to cause shortening.

80. Smooth-muscle relaxation occurs when:

Sources of Cytosolic Calcium

81. Two sources of calcium for initiation of smooth-muscle contraction are:

    a.

    b.

82. In contrast to skeletal muscle, smooth muscle can be graded by varying the cytosolic _____ concentration.

83. Smooth-muscle tone is maintained by:

Membrane Activation

84. List several inputs to smooth-muscle cells that can affect contractility by altering the cytosolic calcium concentration.

    a.

    b.

    c.

    d.

    e.

85. During action potentials in smooth-muscle cells, _____ ions carry positive charges into the cell during depolarization.

86. The spontaneous depolarization to or toward threshold in smooth-muscle cells results in what is known as a(n) _____ potential.

Nerves and hormones

87. Compare the innervation of smooth muscle with the innervation of skeletal muscle.

88. Smooth-muscle cells have receptors on their plasma membranes specific for:

89. Local factors which affect smooth-muscle contractility by affecting cytosolic calcium include:

Types of Smooth Muscle

90. The two main types of smooth muscle are:

    a.

    b.

91. Describe each of the two types of smooth muscle and give examples of where each is found.

Review Table 11-6, page 345.

Review the SUMMARY and REVIEW QUESTIONS at the end of this section and the THOUGHT QUESTIONS at the end of this chapter in your textbook.

CHAPTER 11 ANSWER KEY

1. a. skeletal   b. cardiac   c. smooth

2. A muscle is composed of many muscle fibers (cells) bound together by connective tissue.

3. tendons

4. striated, multinucleated

5. myosin, actin

6. See Fig. 11-5, page 308.

7. six, three

8. cross bridges

9. Contraction is the activation of cross bridges in a muscle fiber, resulting in force generation.

10. The thick and thin filaments in each sarcomere slide over each other, causing sarcomere shortening (and muscle-fiber shortening) with no change in the thick (myosin) or thin (actin) filament length.

11. a. attachment of the cross bridges to the thin filaments
    b. movement of the cross bridges, producing sliding of the filaments
    c. detachment of the cross bridges from the thick filaments
    d. movement of the cross bridges so they can reattach to the thin filaments and repeat the cycle

12. a. The energy from ATP hydrolysis provides the energy for cross-bridge movement.
    b. The binding of ATP to the myosin breaks the cross bridges between the actin and myosin filaments so that another cycle can be repeated.

13. relaxation, dissociation, rigor mortis

14. See Fig. 11-13, page 313.

15. seven

16. tropomyosin

17. calcium

18. See Fig. 11-16, page 316.

19. transverse tubules

20. lateral sacs

21. ATP

22. a. Hydrolysis of ATP by myosin energizes the cross bridges, providing the energy for force generation.
    b. Binding of ATP to myosin dissociates cross bridges bound to actin, allowing the bridges to repeat their cycle of activity.
    c. Hydrolysis of ATP by the Ca-ATPase in the sarcoplasmic reticulum provides the energy for the active transport of calcium ions into the lateral sacs of the reticulum, lowering cytosolic calcium, ending the contraction, and allowing the muscle fiber to relax.

23. skeletal-muscle fibers

24. motor neuron and all the muscle fibers it innervates

25. the region of the muscle-fiber membrane that lies directly under the axon terminal of the motor neuron innervating it

26. the junction of the axon terminal with the motor end plate

27. voltage-sensitive calcium, calcium, acetylcholine (ACh)

28. end-plate, sodium, potassium

29. See Fig. 11-19, page 318.

30. true

31. false

32. acetylcholinesterase, motor end plate

33. a. blocking the acetylcholine receptors (curare)
    b. blocking or inhibiting acetylcholinesterase (nerve gases)
    c. blocking the release of acetylcholine from nerve terminals (toxin from *Clostridium botulinum*)

34. Muscle tension is the force exerted on an object by the contracting muscle. Load is the force exerted on the muscle by the weight.

35. Isometric contraction occurs when a muscle develops tension but does not shorten (constant length). Isotonic contraction occurs when the load on the muscle remains constant but the muscle shortens (constant tension). Lengthening contraction occurs when an unsupported load on a muscle is greater than the tension generated by the cross bridges; the load pulls the muscle to a longer length.

36. muscle tension, the distance the muscle shortens (See Fig. 11-20, page 320.)

37. See Figs. 11-21 and 11-22, page 321.

38. a. b   b. a   c. b

39. summation, tetanus

40. less than

41. See Fig. 11-26, page 323.

42. This is the length where the greatest number of cross bridges are formed.

43. decreases

44. a. phosphorylation of ADP to ATP by creatine phosphate (very rapid)
    b. mitochondrial oxidative phosphorylation of ADP to ATP
    c. glycolysis (ADP to ATP)

45. a. blood glucose   b. muscle glycogen

46. glycogen depletion, increased hydrogen ions due to increased lactic acid, decreased release of calcium from the sarcoplasmic reticulum in response to electrical stimulation, increased organic phosphate concentrations

47. failure of specific cerebral cortical centers to send impulses down the motor neurons to cause muscle fibers to contract

48. low, high

49. high, high

50. high, high

51. larger

52. fast-glycolytic, slow-oxidative

53. muscle fibers, motor units

54. all three

55. slow-oxidative

56. fast-glycolytic

57. a. the amount of tension each fiber develops
    b. the number of fibers contracting

58. a. the number of fibers in each motor unit
    b. the number of active motor units

59. fewer

60. fine

61. more

62. recruitment

63. Atrophy (from muscle disuse or denervation) results in a decrease in the amount of contractile proteins and a decrease in fiber size (diameter). Hypertrophy (from increased use—exercise) results in increased muscle proteins and increased fiber size.

64. do not change

65. fast- and slow-oxidative

66. fast-glycolytic

67. inflammation of the muscles resulting from tissue damage

68. flexion, extension

69. biceps, triceps

70. true

71. a. d   b. a   c. b   d. c

72. the autonomic nervous system

73. less than

74. The filaments are oriented slightly diagonal to the long axis of the cell and are attached to the plasma membrane or cytoplasmic structures by dense bodies. There are no organized myofibrils or regular alignment of filaments into sarcomeres. Therefore, no banding pattern (light and dark bands) is seen in smooth muscle as in skeletal muscle. (See Fig. 11-37, page 339.)

75. one-third, two times

76. true

77. See Fig. 11-39, page 340.

78. calmodulin

79. myosin light-chain kinase

80. The phosphorylated myosin is dephosphorylated by a phosphatase enzyme; or when the rate of dephosphorylation exceeds the rate of phosphorylation of myosin.

81. a. sarcoplasmic reticulum
    b. extracellular calcium entering through plasma membrane calcium channels

82. calcium

83. low levels of cytosolic calcium that maintain a low level of cross-bridge activity

84. a. spontaneous electrical activity in the fiber plasma membrane
    b. neurotransmitters released by autonomic neurons
    c. hormones
    d. locally induced changes in the chemical composition (paracrine agents, acidity, oxygen, osmolarity, and ion concentrations) of the extracellular fluid surrounding the fiber
    e. stretch

85. calcium

86. pacemaker

87. Smooth muscle is innervated by sympathetic or parasympathetic fibers whose branches release neurotransmitters from varicosities. These neurotransmitters may depolarize or hyperpolarize the smooth-muscle membrane, leading to an increase or decrease in cytosolic calcium. Skeletal muscle is innervated by spinal (somatic) nerves, and the neurotransmitter (ACh) is released onto the motor end plate to cause depolarization only.

88. neurotransmitters and a variety of hormones

89. paracrines, acidity, oxygen, osmolarity, ionic composition of the extracellular fluid, stretch

90. a. single-unit smooth muscle
    b. multiunit smooth muscle

91. Single-unit smooth-muscle cells propagate action potentials from one cell to another through gap junctions. A small number of the cells are pacemaker cells that generate and conduct action potentials to cells that are not spontaneously active. Contractility can be altered by nerves, hormones, and local factors, as well as stretch. This type of smooth muscle is found in the intestinal tract, uterus, and small-diameter blood vessels. Multiunit smooth muscle is characterized by few gap junctions, and each muscle fiber responds independently of its neighbor. There is little propagation of electrical activity from fiber to fiber. The contractile activity is closely coupled to nerve activity. These fibers do not respond to stretch nor do they have pacemaker cells.

CHAPTER
12
CONTROL OF BODY MOVEMENT

1. All the motor neurons for a given muscle make up the _____ for that muscle.

MOTOR CONTROL HIERARCHY

2. Describe the functional motor control hierarchy for controlling skeletal-muscle contraction.

3. The motor program ("middle level") is constantly being adjusted by input from:

Voluntary and Involuntary Actions

4. Most motor behavior is (*voluntary, involuntary, combination of both*).

LOCAL CONTROL OF MOTOR NEURONS

Interneurons

5. Most input to motor neurons is from local interneurons which receive input from:

Local Afferent Input

6. Local afferent input to local interneurons brings information from:

Length-monitoring systems and the stretch reflex

7. Draw a muscle spindle. Include stretch receptors, the afferent nerve from the stretch receptors, intrafusal fibers, and extrafusal fibers.

8. As a passive stretch of a muscle activates the muscle-spindle stretch receptors, the firing rate in the afferent nerve is (*increased, decreased*). During contraction of a muscle, the afferent firing rate from the stretch receptors is (*increased, decreased*).

9. Diagram the monosynaptic stretch (myotatic) reflex.

10. Differentiate between a monosynaptic and a polysynaptic reflex.

11. The activation of one muscle and the simultaneous inhibition of its antagonistic muscle is called _____ .

12. Diagram a reflex with interneurons that activate the motor neurons of a synergistic muscle.

13. Muscle responses that are on the same side of the body as the receptors are known as _____ responses, while responses on the opposite side of the body are known as _____ responses.

Alpha-gamma coactivation

14. As extrafusal fibers shorten, intrafusal fibers shorten in order to maintain tension on spindle stretch receptors. (*true, false*)

15. Alpha motor neurons activate _____ fibers, whereas gamma motor neurons activate _____ fibers.

16. Coactivation of alpha and gamma fibers ensures:

Tension-monitoring systems

17. The receptors that monitor how much tension is being exerted by contracting motor units of muscle are called _____ and are located _____ .

18. Increased golgi tendon afferent firing results in (*stimulation, inhibition*) of the motor neurons to the contracting muscle.

THE BRAIN MOTOR CENTERS AND THE DESCENDING PATHWAYS THEY CONTROL

Cerebral Cortex

19. The _____ cortex refers to all parts of the cerebral cortex that act together in the control of muscle movement.

20. The primary motor cortex is associated with:

21. Describe how the neurons for various muscle groups are arranged in the motor cortex.

22. The cortical areas representing the _____ and _____ are largest.

23. The premotor area is associated with:

Subcortical and Brainstem Nuclei

24. The paired basal ganglia (subcortical nuclei) help determine direction, force, and speed of movements and exert (*stimulatory, inhibitory*) influences on the on-going motor control systems. Inadequate functioning of the basal ganglia results in _____ disease.

25. The substantia nigra (subcortical nuclei) release the neurotransmitter _____ to the basal ganglia.

26. Treatments for Parkinson's disease include:

Cerebellum

27. The cerebellum influences:

Descending Pathways

Corticospinal pathway

28. The cell bodies of the corticospinal tracts are located in the _____.

28. The fibers of the corticospinal tract cross over to the opposite side at the level of the _____ and descend to terminate on interneurons at the appropriate level of the spinal cord.

30. Skeletal muscles on the right side of the body are innervated by corticospinal fibers originating from the (*right, left*) cerebal cortex.

31. The corticobulbar pathway begins in the _____ and ends in the _____. This pathway controls _____ .

Noncorticospinal pathways

32. Noncorticospinal pathways go from the _____ to the spinal cord and are important in controlling _____ .

33. The (*corticospinal, noncorticospinal*) tracts have a greater influence over control of fine, coordinated movements such as finger and hand movements, while the (*corticospinal, noncorticospinal*) descending tracts are involved more with upright posture, locomotion, and head and body movements.

MUSCLE TONE

34. Muscle tone is due to:

    a.

    b.

35. Abnormally high muscle tone is known as _____, while abnormally low muscle tone is _____ .

36. Indicate whether the following descriptions are associated with hypertonia (a) or hypotonia (b).

    a. ___ spasticity or rigidity

    b. ___ flaccid state

    c. ___ associated with cerebellar disease or alpha motor neuron or muscle disease

    d. ___ associated with disorders of descending pathways

MAINTENANCE OF UPRIGHT POSTURE AND BALANCE

37. The center of gravity for an erect human is _____ .

38. Afferent information for postural reflexes comes from:

39. Efferent information from postural reflexes is carried via the _____ neurons to _____ .

40. Examples of postural reflexes are:

    a.

    b.

WALKING

41. The cyclic, alternating movements of walking are controlled by networks of inter-neurons called _____, which are located in the _____.

42. Input into the neurons involved in walking comes from:

Review the SUMMARY, REVIEW QUESTIONS, and THOUGHT QUESTIONS at the end of this chapter in your textbook.

CHAPTER 12 ANSWER KEY

1. motor neuron pool

2. Highest level: "command" neurons form complex plans (association cortex, areas involved with memory and emotion, supplementary motor area).
   Middle level: generates a "motor program" required to perform a movement; program is transmitted by descending pathways to the lowest control level (sensorimotor cortex, cerebellum, parts of basal ganglia, some brainstem nuclei).
   Lowest level ("local level"): motor neurons to muscles from the brainstem or spinal cord.

3. receptors in eyes, vestibular apparatus, muscles, tendons, joints, and skin.

4. combination of both

5. peripheral receptors, descending pathways, other interneurons

6. muscles controlled by the motor neurons; other nearby muscles; tendons, joints, and skin surrounding the muscle

7. See Fig. 12-4, page 354.

8. increased, decreased

9. See Fig. 12-6, page 356.

10. A monosynaptic reflex has no interneurons between the afferent (sensory) and efferent (motor) neurons. A polysynaptic reflex has one or more interneurons between the afferent and efferent neurons involved in the reflex.

11. reciprocal innervation

12. See Fig. 12-9, page 358.

13. ipsilateral, contralateral

14. true

15. extrafusal, intrafusal

16. continuous information about muscle length so that moment-to-moment adjustments can be made

17. golgi tendon organs, in the tendons near their junction with the muscle

18. inhibition

19. sensorimotor

20. movements involving the use of individual muscle groups, e.g., those that move a finger or toe.

21. The neurons for the muscle groups are arranged from the top of the brain moving down the motor cortex: toes, feet, leg, trunk, arm, hand, fingers, neck, and face.

22. hands, face

23. more complicated motor functions such as change in force or velocity of a movement, a spoken command, two-handed coordinations, etc., and an important gateway for relaying processed information from other regions of the cerebral cortex to the primary motor area or to descending pathways

24. inhibitory, Parkinson's

25. dopamine

26. L-dopa (a precursor of dopamine), Deprenyl (an inhibitor of the brain enzyme that breaks down dopamine), transplantation of fetal neurons that release dopamine

27. posture, movement, and learning of motor skills

28. cerebral cortex (sensorimotor region)

29. medulla

30. left

31. sensorimotor cortex, brainstem, motor neurons that innervate muscles of the eyes, face, tongue, and throat

32. brainstem; upright posture, balance, and walking

33. corticospinal, noncorticospinal

34. a. viscoelastic properties of muscles and joints
    b. alpha motor neuron activity

35. hypertonia, hypotonia

36. a. a   b. b   c. b   d. a

37. just above the pelvis

38. eyes, vestibular apparatus, and proprioceptors

39. alpha motor, skeletal muscle

40. a. a stretch reflex
    b. a crossed-extensor reflex

41. central pattern generators, spinal cord

42. descending pathways, eyes, ears, vestibular apparatus, and proprioception

CHAPTER
13
CONSCIOUSNESS AND BEHAVIOR

STATES OF CONSCIOUSNESS

1. State of consciousness refers to:

Electroencephalogram

2. What kind of electric potentials are recorded by an electroencephalogram (EEG)?

3. The four major frequencies (waves) of an EEG and their corresponding states of consciousness are:

4. The "rhythm generators" for the waves of an EEG are thought to originate from the _____, which sends a fluctuating output through neurons to the _____.

The Waking State

5. The alpha rhythm of an EEG with a frequency of about _____ Hz is associated with _____.

6. The beta rhythm of an EEG with a frequency of about _____ Hz is associated with _____.

Sleep

7. The two phases of sleep are:

   a.

   b.

8. How does the EEG pattern for these two phases of sleep differ?

9. It normally takes about _____ minutes to progress from stage 1 to stage 4 slow-wave sleep, and then the process reverses itself.

10. Dreaming usually occurs during (*slow-wave, REM*) sleep.

11. It is easiest to awake oneself during (*slow-wave, REM*) sleep.

12. Describe how a typical night's sleep would appear with regard to the frequency of sleep cycles.

13. Some physiological functions that occur during slow-wave sleep include:

14. Some physiological functions that occur during REM sleep include:

Neural Substrates of States of Consciousness

15. The normal sleep-wake cycle is about _____ h awake and _____ h asleep.

16. The sleep-wake rhythm is controlled by the _____ and is affected by the preoptic area that _____ and the posterior hypothalamus that _____. The differential effects of these areas on sleep is due to the release of different types of the same neurotransmitter, _____.

17. The brainstem also has neurons involved in the sleep-wake cycle affecting _____, _____ and _____. Neurotransmitters involved in these areas include _____.

18. During infections, there is an increase in the cytokine _____, which also affects sleep; this may be why we sleep more when we are sick.

Coma and Brain Death

19. Differentiate between coma and brain death.

CONSCIOUS EXPERIENCES

Directed Attention

20. Define:
    a. Directed attention:

    b. Orienting response:

c. Preattentive processing:

d. Habituation:

Neural mechanisms for directed attention

21. The three distinct neurological processes involved in directed attention are:

    a.

    b.

    c.

22. The lobes of the brain most involved in directed attention are the _____ lobes, especially in the (*right, left*) hemisphere.

23. The brain structure involved in directed attention which seems to determine which areas of the brain gain predominance in the stream-of-conscious experience is the _____.

Neural Mechanisms for Conscious Experiences

24. What are some events that are required for a conscious experience to occur?

25. What parts of the brain might be involved in a "temporary set" of neurons eliciting a conscious experience?

MOTIVATION AND EMOTION

Motivation

26. Primary motivated behavior is behavior that _____ .

27. The area of the brain involved in primary motivational behavior is the _____ .

28. Chemical mediators involved in motivation and positive reward systems are:

Emotion

29. Differentiate between inner emotion and emotional behavior.

30. The area of the brain that integrates the inner emotions with emotional behavior is the _____ system.

ALTERED STATES OF CONSCIOUSNESS

31. Schizophrenia is caused in part by overstimulation of _____ receptors.

32. Affective disorders are characterized by _____ and include such disorders as _____ . These disorders are caused in part by disturbances in the neurotransmitter _____ .

33. Classical antidepressant drugs act to increase the concentrations of _____ and/or _____ at synaptic sites.

34. Psychoactive drugs used to deliberately elevate moods (euphorigens) exert their effects by _____ .

35. Drug tolerance can develop as a result of:

LEARNING AND MEMORY

36. Differentiate between learning and memory.

37. The two types of memory are:

    a.

    b.

38. The process of transferring memories from working to long-term is called
    _____.

39. Working memory is carried out in the _____ lobes of the cerebral cortex and
    depends on the neurotransmitter _____.

40. Working memory is very important in attention focusing and in memory-based skills.
    (*true, false*)

41. The two types of long-term memory are:

    a.

    b.

The Location of Memory

42. The brain structures most involved in memory are:

The Neural Basis of Learning and Memory

43. (*Working, long-term*) memory is affected by coma, deep anesthesia, electroconvulsive shock, and lack of blood supply to the brain—all of which interfere with the electrical activity of the brain.

44. (*Working, long-term*) memory is associated with "enriched environment"—induced anatomical changes especially in the cerebral cortex, hippocampus, and cerebellum.

CEREBRAL DOMINANCE AND LANGUAGE

45. In 90 percent of the population, the (*right, left*) cerebral hemisphere is dominant in producing language and in performing other tasks that require rapid changes over time.

46. Lobes of the cerebral cortex involved in language include:

47. Verbal memories are primarily associated with the (*right, left*) cerebral hemisphere, and nonverbal memories are primarily associated with the (*right, left*).

Review the SUMMARY, REVIEW QUESTIONS, and THOUGHT QUESTIONS at the end of this chapter in your textbook.

CHAPTER 13 ANSWER KEY

1. whether a person is awake, asleep, drowsy, etc., and can be measured by an electro-encephalogram

2. EEG patterns are due primarily to graded postsynaptic potentials, not to action potentials. These are very low-voltage potentials (microvolt range) and frequencies of 1 to 30 Hz (cycles/s).

3. Alpha: 8 to 13 Hz, awake, relaxed, eyed closed; beta: 13 to 25 Hz, awake, alert; delta: 0.5 to 4 Hz, sleep, stages 3 to 4; theta: 4 to 8 Hz, sleep, stages 3 to 4

4. thalamus, cerebral cortex

5. 5 to 13, an awake, relaxed state with eyes closed

6. 13 to 25, an awake, alert state as in being attentive to a stimulus or thinking hard about something

7. a. slow-wave sleep
   b. paradoxical (REM) sleep

8. In slow-wave sleep, the EEG progresses through four stages (stages 1 to 4) characterized by slower-frequency, higher-amplitude waves, with stage 4 being deep sleep. In paradoxical (REM) sleep, the EEG is similar to that of the alert, awake state (high frequency and low amplitude).

9. 30 to 45

10. REM

11. REM

12. There would be four to five cycles of stage 1/stage 4/stage 1 sleep (each lasting about 90 to 100 min) with regular intervals of REM sleep. Slow-wave sleep cycles constitute 75 to 80 percent of the sleep time.

13. pulsatile release of growth hormone and gonadotropic hormones from the anterior pituitary; decrease in blood pressure, heart rate, and respiratory rate

14. increase and irregularity in blood pressure, heart rate, and respiratory rate; erection of penis, engorgement of clitoris; facial and limb muscle twitches

15. 16, 8

16. suprachiasmic nucleus in the hypothalamus, promotes sleep, causes wakefulness, prostaglandins

17. arousal, slow-wave sleep, REM sleep; serotonin, dopamine, norepinephrine, and acetylcholine

18. interleukin-1

19. Coma is described as a severe or total decrease in mental function with no arousal even in response to vigorous stimulation. Eyes are closed. There are no sleep-wake cycles. Comas are often reversible. Brain death is the irreversible loss of all brain functions. The general criteria for determining brain death are listed in Table 13-2, page 375.

20. a. avoiding distractions from irrelevant stimuli while seeking out and focusing on stimuli that are important
    b. behavior that causes a person to orient toward the stimulus source
    c. processing by the brain that focuses attention only toward stimuli that are meaningful
    d. progressive decrease in response to a repeated stimulus

21. a. attention must be disengaged from the present focus
    b. attention must be moved to the new focus
    c. attention must be engaged at the new focus

22. parietal, right

23. locus coeruleus

24. graded potentials or action potentials in some part of the brain, a set of neurons temporarily functioning together in a specific way, synchronous activity of the neurons in the "temporary set" leading to or is the conscious awareness of what we see, neurons involved in the synchronous activity shift and a different "temporary set" may be involved, occurrence of interacting neuronal networks occur

25. cerebral cortex, thalamus, basal ganglia

26. is directly related to satisfying homeostatic needs (thirst, hunger, etc.)

27. lateral hypothalamus

28. norepinephrine and dopamine or drugs that increase activity in the catecholamine pathways (amphetamines)

29. Inner emotions are feelings within a person (fear, anger, joy). Emotional behavior is the outward expression and display of inward feelings (attack, crying, blushing)

30. limbic

31. dopamine

32. serious mood disorders and swings; depressions, manias, bipolar affective disorders; norepinephrine

33. serotonin, norepinephrine

34. altering neurotransmitter-receptor interactions

35. drugs stimulating an increased synthesis of enzymes that degrade the drug, thus more drug is needed for the same effect; changes in the number and/or sensitivity of the receptors that respond to the drug

36. Learning is the acquisition and storage of information as a consequence of experience. Memory is the relatively permanent storage form of learned information.

37. a. working memory (limited capacity, short-term, seconds to minutes)
    b. long-term memory (unlimited capacity, lasts for hours, days, years)

38. memory consolidation

39. frontal, dopamine

40. true

41. a. procedural (*how* to do something)
    b. declarative (remembering facts and events)

42. hippocampus (declarative learning), areas of the cerebral cortex closely associated with the limbic system (declarative learning), cerebellum (procedural learning), amygdala (pain avoidance learning)

43. working

44. long-term

45. left

46. frontal, parietal, temporal

47. left, right

CHAPTER
14
CIRCULATION

Section A. Blood

1. Blood is composed of:

   a.

   b.

2. Three types of cells or fragments of cells in blood are:

   a.

   b.

   c.

3. The major function of each of the above cell types is:

4. Calculate the hematocrit (hct) for an individual whose blood has been "spun down" in a hematocrit tube. The formed elements compose 4 mm and the plasma 6 mm of this tube.

5. The normal hematocrit value for a female is _____, and for a male is _____ .

6. If the total blood volume is 5 L for the individual whose hematocrit you determined in the previous question, calculate this person's erythrocyte volume: _____ and plasma volume: _____ . Show your work here.

PLASMA

7. The three major proteins in plasma are:

   a.

   b.

   c.

8. The most abundant type of plasma protein is: _____

9. Serum is: _____

10. Other components in plasma include: _____

11. The normal color of plasma is _____ as a result of hemoglobin break-down products called _____ .

BLOOD CELLS

Erythrocytes

12. Draw an erythrocyte and indicate the diameter in micrometers. (Pay special attention to the shape.)

13. Why is this shape advantageous?

14. The most abundant protein in erythrocytes is _____ .

15. There are approximately _____ molecules of hemoglobin in each erythrocyte.

16. Diagram a hemoglobin molecule and label its parts.

17. The atom present in each heme group is _____ .

18. Each heme molecule can bind to _____ molecule(s) of oxygen.

19. A normal hemoglobin value for females is _____ , and for males is _____ .
    (Be sure to include units!)

20. Erythrocytes are produced in _____ .

21. Mature human erythrocytes (*do, do not*) have nuclei.

22. How do reticulocytes differ from mature erythrocytes?

23. The average life span of an erythrocyte is approximately _____ days.

24. Erythrocytes are destroyed in the _____ and _____ .

25. What happens to the iron when erythrocytes are destroyed?

26. The major breakdown product of heme is _____ .

Iron

27. What is iron's role in erythrocytes?

28. List some dietary sources of iron.

29. How does dietary iron become available to erythrocytes?

30. Iron is stored in the body in the _____ in a protein called _____ .

31. The iron-transport protein in plasma is _____ .

Folic acid and vitamin B$_{12}$

32. Folic acid is necessary for erythrocyte production because it _____ .

33. Vitamin B$_{12}$ is necessary for erythrocyte production because it _____ .

34. Why may a strict vegetarian be deficient in vitamin B$_{12}$?

Regulation of erythrocyte production (erythropoiesis)

35. Diagram the sequence of events for erythropoiesis. Include the kidney, the hormone erythropoietin, and the bone marrow.

36. _____ increases erythropoietin release from the kidneys.

Anemia

37. Define anemia.

38. List four different causes of anemia.

   a.

   b.

   c.

   d.

39. Define polycythemia.

Leukocytes

40. Define polymorphonuclear (PMN) granulocytes.

41. List the three types of PMN granulocytes.

    a.

    b.

    c.

42. List two leukocyte types that have no (or very few) granules in their cytoplasm.

    a.

    b.

43. Of the five leukocyte types, which is the most numerous? _____

44. Where are granular leukocytes made? _____

45. Where are agranular leukocytes made? _____

Platelets

46. Are circulating platelets fragments of cells or whole cells? _____

47. What is the major function of platelets? _____

Regulation of Blood Cell Production

48. List the major bones of an adult that are involved in blood cell production.

49. The name of the bone marrow cells that give rise to precursors of all the blood cell types is _____ .

50. Protein hormones (12 or more) involved in blood cell production are collectively termed _____ .

51. List three of these protein hormones.

    a.

    b.

    c.

52. List the following clinical values: (Be sure to include units.)

    a. Erythrocytes:

    b. Leukocytes:

    c. Platelets:

    d. Hematocrit:

    e. Hemoglobin:

Review the SECTION SUMMARY and the REVIEW QUESTIONS at the end of this section in your textbook.

Section B. Overall Design of the Cardiovascular System

53. Gases, nutrients, and metabolic end products move from the capillaries to all cells of the body (or from the cells to the capillaries) by processes known as _____ and _____ .

54. Approximately _____ percent of the total circulating blood volume is present in the capillaries.

55. Diagram the heart, labeling the four chambers. Draw arrows to indicate how blood flows through these four chambers. (*Remember:* The right pump and the left pump are not in direct communication with each other.)

56. Fill in the blanks to indicate the flow of blood:

Right atrium
⬇
a. _____
⬇
Pulmonary circulation (lungs)
⬇
b. _____
⬇
c. _____
⬇
Systemic circulation (body)

57. Vessels that carry blood from the heart are called _____.

58. Vessels that carry blood from the lungs and return it back to the heart are called _____

59. List the vessels through which blood passes as it flows from the left ventricle and returns to the right atrium:

Left ventricle ➡ _____ ➡ _____ ➡ _____ ➡ _____ ➡ _____ ➡ _____ right atrium

60. The large vein that collects blood from the upper part of the body is the _____.

61. The large vein that collects blood from the lower part of the body is the _____. Both of these veins empty into the _____.

62. Blood going to the lungs has a (*high, low*) oxygen content.

63. Blood coming from the lungs has a (*high, low*) oxygen content.

64. All blood returning from the systemic veins is (*oxygenated, deoxygenated*) before returning to the systemic arteries.

65. All blood flowing from the pulmonary arteries to the pulmonary veins is (*oxygenated, deoxygenated*) as it passes through the lungs.

66. All blood pumped by the right heart goes to the _____.

67. All blood pumped by the left heart goes to the _____.

PRESSURE, FLOW, AND RESISTANCE

68. Write the equation that relates pressure, flow, and resistance.

69. In your own words, state what this equation says.

70. For the equation $R = \eta L8/r^4$, identify the following:
    a. $R =$
    b. $\eta =$
    c. $l =$
    d. $r =$

71. Based on the above equation, if η increases (as the result of an increased hematocrit for example), R will (*increase, decrease*). If r increases, R will (*increase, decrease*).

72. Of the three major factors that affect resistance to blood flow (η, L, r), which is most important?

73. Increasing the radius of a vessel 2-fold will decrease its resistance _____ -fold.

Review the SECTION SUMMARY and REVIEW QUESTIONS at the end of this section in your textbook.

Section C. The Heart

ANATOMY

74. The fibrous sac surrounding the heart is the _____.

75. The thick wall of the heart composed primarily of cardiac muscle is called the _____.

76. The thin layer of cells lining the cardiac chambers is the _____ .

77. Diagram the heart, labeling the four valves. Draw arrows to indicate the direction of blood flow through the heart.

78. List the cardiac valves:

AV valves	Semilunar valves
a. _____	c. _____
b. _____	d. _____

79. The papillary muscles are attached to the _____ valves by fibrous strands called _____ .

Review Fig. 14-14, page 410, in your textbook.

Cardiac Muscle

80. Compare and contrast cardiac muscle with skeletal and smooth muscle.

81. Special cardiac-muscle cells are modified to form a special conducting network known as the _____ .

82. The peptide hormone secreted by special atrial muscle cells is _____ .

Innervation

83. Cardiac muscle is innervated by both divisions of the autonomic nervous system. Fill in the blanks:

Divisions of the ANS	Postganglionic transmitter released	Receptors on cardiac muscle
a. _____	c. _____	e. _____
b. _____	d. _____	f. _____

Blood supply

84. The _____ arteries supply oxygen-rich blood to the myocardium.

HEARTBEAT COORDINATION

Cardiac Action Potentials

85. Identify:

    A:

    B:

    C:

    D:

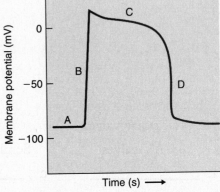

Ventricular muscle action potential

86. Describe the membrane permeability changes occurring at the following letters on the action potential above:

    B:

    C:

    D:

87. Draw a ventricular muscle-cell action potential and an atrial muscle-cell action potential.

Ventricular muscle-cell AP   Atrial muscle-cell AP

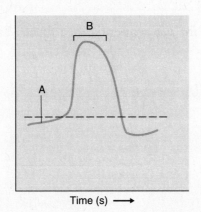

Time (s) ⟶

88. In the figure above, the gradual depolarization, A, is known as the _____.
    B is the _____.

89. This unstable resting membrane potential, A, is the cause of _____.

90. The firing rate of the SA node in humans is about _____ beats/min.

91. Membrane permeability changes of the following ions responsible for *generation* of the
    pacemaker potential at the SA node are:
    a. P_{Na^+}: (*increase, decrease, no change*)
    b. P_{K^+}: (*increase, decrease, no change*)
    c. $P_{Ca^{2+}}$: (*increase, decrease, no change*)

Sequence of Excitation

92. The pacemaker of the heart resides in the _____ cells.

93. Draw the electrical conducting system of the heart.

94. The greatest delay in the electrical conducting system of the heart occurs in the
    _____.

The Electrocardiogram

95. Draw a typical ECG tracing for *two* sequential heartbeats. Label the P, QRS, and T waves.

96. The P wave represents _____ .

97. The QRS complex represents _____ .

98. The T wave represents _____ .

99. Draw an ECG tracing with a ventricular muscle-cell action potential below it. (Be sure the ventricular depolarization and repolarization occur at the same time for *both* tracings!)

100. An ECG provides information concerning the (*electrical, mechanical*) events of the heart.

Excitation-Contraction Coupling

101. List in order the sequence of events by which the action potential causes increased release of calcium from the sarcoplasmic reticulum.

    a.

    b.

    c.

    d.

Refractory Period of the Heart

102. Define refractory period.

103. Draw a ventricular muscle action potential and label its refractory period. (Cardiac muscle has a refractory period of 250 ms, and skeletal muscle has a refractory period of 1 to 2 ms.)

104. Based upon your understanding of refractory period, explain why cardiac muscle cannot be tetanized.

MECHANICAL EVENTS OF THE CARDIAC CYCLE

105. The phase of the cardiac cycle that represents ventricular contraction is _____. The phase that represents ventricular relaxation is _____.

106. Ventricular contraction and blood ejection (approx. 0.3 s) represents: _____.

107. Ventricular relaxation and blood filling (approx. 0.5 s) represents: _____.

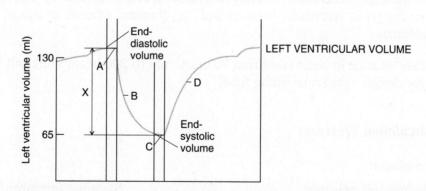

108. Identify the following from the left ventricular volume curve:

    A:

    B:

    C:

    D:

109. What part(s) of the above ventricular volume curve occur(s) during systole? _____ Diastole? _____

110. The volume represented by the line labeled X above is called _____.

111. In an individual at rest, _____ percent of ventricular filling occurs *before* atrial contraction.

Mid-to-Late Diastole

112. During ventricular diastole, the _____ valves are closed and the _____ valves are open.

113. The amount of blood in the ventricle at the end of diastole is called _____. This volume is approximately _____ ml.

Systole

114. As ventricular pressure increases, the _____ valves close and the _____ valves open.

115. The amount of blood remaining in the ventricle at the end of ejection is called the _____. This volume is approximately _____ ml.

116. End diastolic volume – end systolic volume = _____.

Early Diastole

117. The isovolumetric ventricular relaxation period is characterized by a(n) (*increase, decrease, no change*) in ventricular pressure and a(n) (*increase, decrease, no change*) in ventricular volume.

118. A significant increase in heart rate (from 70 beats/min to 200 beats/min) will (*increase, decrease, not change*) ventricular filling time.

Pulmonary Circulation Pressures

119. Fill in the blanks:

Pulmonary pressures

Systemic pressures

a. Systolic _____ mmHg

c. Systolic _____ mmHg

b. Diastolic _____ mmHg

d. Diastolic _____ mmHg

120. Right ventricular stroke volume is normally _____ ml.

121. Left ventricular stroke volume is normally _____ml.

122. How does the anatomy of the right ventricular wall correlate with the low-pressure pulmonary circulation?

Heart Sounds

123. The first heart sound (lub) is due to _____.

124. The second heart sound (dup) is due to _____.

CARDIAC OUTPUT

125. Define cardiac output (CO):

126. CO = HR × _____.

127. At rest, a cardiac output of ____ L/min = 72 beats/min × ___ ml/beat.

128. During exercise, if heart rate increases to 80 beats/min and stroke volume increases to 120 ml/beat, the CO will be _____. (Be sure to include units.)

Control of Heart Rate

129. (*With, without*) neural innervation, the heart rate at rest is approx. 100 beats/min.

130. Parasympathetic innervation (*increases, decreases, does not change*) heart rate.

131. Sympathetic innervation (*increases, decreases, does not change*) heart rate.

132. In the resting state, the heart rate is predominately under (*parasympathetic, sympathetic*) innervation.

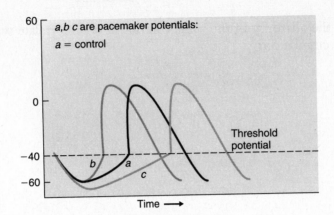

SA-nodal action potential

133. _____ represents parasympathetic stimulation.

134. _____ represents sympathetic stimulation.

Control of Stroke Volume

135. Define stroke volume (SV). (*Remember:* The ventricles never completely empty during contraction.)

136. Two factors that change SV are:

    a.

    b.

137. Define Starling's law of the heart:

The sympathetic nerves

138. Sympathetic nerves release the neurotransmitter _____ , which interacts with the _____ receptors on the myocardium to _____ ventricular contractility.

139. Ejection fraction (EF) = $\dfrac{?}{EDV}$ = ___ %

140. EF (*increases, decreases*) with an increase in myocardial contractility.

Review the SECTION SUMMARY and REVIEW QUESTIONS at the end of this section in your textbook.

Section D. The Vascular System

ARTERIES

Arterial Blood Pressure

141. The formula for compliance is: $C =$ _____.

142. Is compliance greater in the arteries or in the veins? _____

143. How is compliance altered in people who have "hardening of the arteries"?

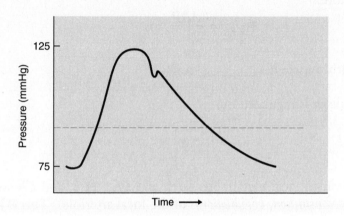

Aortic pressure tracing

144. The systolic pressure (SP) in the above graph is _____.

145. The diastolic pressure (DP) in the above graph is _____.

146. Pulse pressure (PP) = SP – _____.

147. The pulse pressure in the above graph is _____.

148. The magnitude of the pulse pressure is a function of:
    a.
    b.

149. An increase in SV will result in a(n) (*increase, decrease, no change*) in PP.

150. An increase in arterial compliance will result in a(n) (*increase, decrease, no change*) in PP.

151. Arteriosclerosis (hardening of the arteries) will (*increase, decrease, not change*) PP.

152. MAP = DP + 1/3 _____

153. Determine the MAP of an individual with a blood pressure of 210/160 mmHg:

_____

Measurement of Arterial Pressure

154. Describe how you can determine your systolic and diastolic blood pressure using a sphygmomanometer.

ARTERIOLES

155. Arterioles are the major vessels that distribute variable amounts of blood to individual organs. Therefore:

$$F_{organ} = \frac{MAP}{?}$$

156. Vascular smooth muscle has _____ tone.

157. Arteriolar diameter is regulated by:

    a.

    b.

158. An accumulation of local metabolites such as CO_2, H^+, and adenosine, or an O_2 lack cause (*vasoconstriction, vasodilation*) of the local arterioles. This is known as active

    _____.

159. In flow autoregulation, when blood flow to an organ is reduced, there is arteriolar (*vasoconstriction, vasodilation*) in an attempt to return blood flow to normal.

160. According to the theory of reactive hyperemia, occlusion of blood flow to an organ or tissue will result in a(n) (*increase, decrease*) in blood flow to that organ when the occlusion is released.

Extrinsic Controls

161. The smooth muscle of arterioles is innervated by sympathetic postganglionic nerve fibers which release _____ which interacts with_____receptors on the arterioles.

162. Indicate whether the following events result in vasoconstriction (VC) or vasodilation (VD):

    a. _____ increased sympathetic firing to vascular smooth muscle

    b. _____ decreased sympathetic firing to vascular smooth muscle

    c. _____ epinephrine (interacting with alpha receptors)

    d. _____ angiotensin II

    e. _____ vasopressin

    f. _____ ANF

Endothelial Cells and Vascular Smooth Muscle

163. Indicate if the following endothelial derived factors cause vasoconstriction (VC) or vasodilation (VD).

   a. _____ prostacyclin

   b. _____ EDRF

   c. _____ endothelin-1

Review Fig. 14-44, page 437, and Table 14-7, page 436.

CAPILLARIES

164. What percent of the circulating blood volume is located in the capillaries? _____

165. List the major functions of the capillaries.

166. The diameter of a capillary is (*greater than, equal to, less than*) the diameter of a red blood cell and is (*greater than, equal to, less than*) the diameter of a human hair.

Anatomy of the Capillary Network

167. Describe the following:

   a. Capillary wall:

   b. Metarterioles:

   c. Precapillary sphincter:

Velocity of Capillary Blood Flow

168. Velocity of blood flow $= \dfrac{1}{\text{total cross-sectional area}}$.

Using the above equation, explain how the velocity of blood flow varies in the arteries, capillaries, and veins.

Diffusion Across the Capillary Wall:
Exchange of Nutrients and Metabolic End Products

169. Three basic mechanisms by which most substances move across the capillary walls are:

    a.

    b.

    c.

170. Nutrients diffuse across the capillary wall into the _____ fluid and then into _____.

171. Metabolic end products diffuse across cells' membranes into the _____ and then into _____.

172. Glucose, oxygen, and carbon dioxide move down their _____ gradient.

173. Describe Starling's law of capillaries. (Include the four forces that can lead to filtration or absorption in the capillary.)

VEINS

174. Explain the statement: Veins are low-resistance conduits for blood flow from the tissues to the heart.

175. The mean pressure in the following vessels is:

    a. Arteries: _____

    b. Capillaries: _____

    c. Veins: _____

176. Why do veins have valves?

Determinants of Venous Pressure

177. Enter A if the description applies to arteries and V if the description applies to veins.

    a. _____ greater compliance

    b. _____ higher pressure

    c. _____ larger volume

178. Veins are innervated by the _____ division of the autonomic nervous system.

179. Three mechanisms that increase venous pressure and venous return are:

    a.

    b.

    c.

180. What is the relationship between venous return and cardiac output?

THE LYMPHATIC SYSTEM

181. The lymphatic system is made up of small organs called _____, tubes called _____ , and a fluid called _____ .

182. Lymph vessels return their fluid to _____ .

183. Lymph vessels have valves. (*true, false*)

184. Lymph fluid is an ultrafiltrate from the _____ .

185. If the lymph vessels are occluded by infection, there is an accumulation of interstitial fluid. This condition is known as _____ .

Mechanism of Lymph Flow

186. Lymphatics exert a pumplike action by inherent rhythmic contractions of _____ muscle in the lymphatic vessel walls.

187. Lymph flow is aided by _____ and _____ pumps.

Review the SECTION SUMMARY and REVIEW QUESTIONS at the end of this section in your textbook.

Section E. Integration of Cardiovascular Function: Regulation of Systemic Arterial Pressure

188. Fill in the blanks and identify:

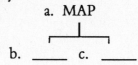

a. MAP

b. _____ c. _____

a.

b.

c.

BARORECEPTOR REFLEXES

Arterial Baroreceptors

189. The arterial baroreceptors are located in the:

a.

b.

190. Diagram on the figure on the right where these arterial baroreceptors are located. Label the major arteries.

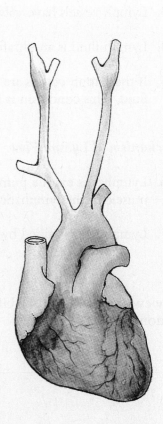

191. Draw the afferent nerves from the baroreceptors to the medulla oblongata on the above diagram. Label these nerves (glossopharyngeal and vagus).

192. If pressure in the arterial baroreceptors increases, the afferent firing of the baro-receptor nerves (*increases, decreases*).

The Medullary Cardiovascular Center and Operation of the Baroreceptor Reflex

193. Draw arrows to complete the following:

                                                        Parasympathetic   Heart

    Arterial baroreceptors   Medullary cardiovascular center

                                                        Sympathetic   Heart
                                                                               Arterioles
                                                                               Veins

194. Fill in the blanks: I = increase, D = decrease

                                          __Parasympathetic firing

    ⬆MAP➡ __Baroreceptor firing ➡ Medulla ⬍ __ CO and __ TPR and __ MAP

                                          __Sympathetic firing

                                          __Parasympathetic firing

    ⬇MAP➡ __Baroreceptor firing ➡ Medulla ⬍ __ CO and __ TPR and __ MAP

                                          __Sympathetic firing

195. This baroreceptor reflex is a (*short, long*)-term regulator of arterial blood pressure.

LONG-TERM REGULATION OF ARTERIAL BLOOD PRESSURE

196. The major factor for long-term regulation of blood pressure is _____.

197. According to long-term regulation of arterial blood pressure, an increase in blood pressure will lead to a(n) (*increase, decrease*) in blood volume, which will lead to a(n) (*increase, decrease*) in blood pressure.

198. According to long-term regulation of arterial blood pressure, a decrease in blood pressure will lead to a(n) (*increase, decrease*) in blood volume, which will lead to a(n) (*increase, decrease*) in blood pressure.

Review the SECTION SUMMARY and REVIEW QUESTIONS at the end of this section in your textbook.

Section F. Cardiovascular Patterns in Health and Disease

Hemorrhage and Other Causes of Hypotension

199. Immediately following a moderate hemorrhage, do the following increase (I), decrease (D), or not change (NC):

a. _____ baroreceptor firing

b. _____ stroke volume

c. _____ heart rate

d. _____ total peripheral resistance

e. _____ cardiac output

f. _____ mean arterial pressure

200. What happens to plasma volume within 12 to 24 h after a moderate hemorrhage?

Shock

201. Shock involves any situation in which there is a(n) (*increase, decrease*) in blood flow to organs or tissues resulting in severe damage.

THE UPRIGHT POSTURE

202. Why do your feet swell during prolonged standing?

203. Why might you faint after standing at attention for a long time?

EXERCISE

204. Indicate if there would be an increase (I) or decrease (D) in each of the following during moderate exercise:

a. _____ blood flow to exercising skeletal muscle

b. _____ blood flow to the skin

c. _____ blood flow to the heart

d. _____ blood flow to the kidneys

e. _____ blood flow to the *gi* tract

f. _____ cardiac output

g. _____ venous return

HYPERTENSION

205. Define hypertension:

206. Differentiate between primary and renal hypertension.

207. List some risk factors associated with primary hypertension.

208. Types of drugs used in treating hypertension that reduce the workload on the heart or reduce TPR are:

HEART FAILURE

209. Draw the Starling curve for a normal heart and indicate how this curve "shifts" for a failing heart.

210. In uncompensated heart failure, what happens to ventricular volume? _____
Ventricular contractility? _____

211. Explain how heart failure can lead to:
    a. Systemic edema:

    b. Pulmonary edema:

212. Explain how the following aid in the treatment of hypertension:
    a. Salt restriction:
    b. Diuretics:
    c. Vasodilator drugs:

CORONARY ARTERY DISEASE

213. The coronary arteries supply blood to _____ .

214. Define:
    a. Angina pectoris:

    b. Myocardial infarction (MI):

    c. Arteriosclerosis:

    d. Atherosclerosis:

215. Explain how the following aid in the treatment of coronary heart disease:
    a. Nitroglycerin:

    b. Beta adrenergic blockers:

    c. Calcium channel blockers:

    d. Blood clot inhibitors:

216. Define:
    a. Stroke:

    b. Embolism:

Review the SUMMARY and REVIEW QUESTIONS at the end of this section and the THOUGHT QUESTIONS at the end of this chapter in your textbook.

CHAPTER 14 ANSWER KEY

1. a. cells   b. plasma

2. a. erythrocytes   b. leukocytes   c. platelets

3. Erythrocytes are the oxygen-carrying cells of the blood. Leukocytes protect against infections and diseases. Platelets function in blood clotting.

4. Hct = 4 mm/10 mm = 40 percent

5. 42 percent, 45 percent

6. 2.0 L, 3.0 L
   Erythrocyte volume = hct × blood volume = $0.4 \times 5.0 = 2.0$ L
   Plasma volume = blood volume − erythrocyte volume = 5 L − 2 L = 3 L

7. a. albumins   b. globulins   c. fibrinogen

8. albumins

9. plasma minus the clotting factors

10. proteins, nutrients, metabolic waste products, electrolytes

11. straw color, bilirubin

12. 7 μm, biconcave disk. See Fig. 14-2, page 396.

13. allows for great flexibility and folding as well as a great surface-to-volume ratio allowing for greater gas diffusion

14. hemoglobin

15. 200 to 300 million

16. See Fig. 14-3, page 398.

17. iron (Fe)

18. four

19. 14 g/dl, 16 g/dl

20. bone morrow

21. do not

22. Reticulocytes have ribosomes that produce a weblike appearance. These are immature cells. Mature erythrocytes lose these ribosomes as well as nuclei.

23. 120

24. spleen, liver

25. The iron is saved and reused in further erythropoiesis or erythrocyte production.

26. bilirubin

27. Iron is the element to which oxygen binds.

28. a. meat   c. shellfish   e. beans
    b. liver   d. egg yolk   f. nuts

29. Dietary iron is absorbed in the intestinal epithelium.

30. liver, ferritin

31. transferrin

32. is needed for DNA formation and normal cell division

33. is required for folic acid action

34. Vitamin B$_{12}$ is found only in animal products, which a strict vegetarian does not eat.

35. See Fig. 14-5, page 400.

36. decreased O$_2$ and testosterone

37. Anemia is a decrease in the total number of erythrocytes, a decreased concentration of hemoglobin per erythrocyte, or a combination of both.

38. a. iron deficiency
    b. blood loss
    c. sickle cell
    d. bone morrow depression from toxic drugs or cancer
    (See Table 14.2, page 400.)

39. Polycythemia is a condition characterized by overproduction of erythrocytes.

40. PMNs are leukocytes with multilobed nuclei and many membrane-bound granules.

41. a. eosinophils   b. basophils   c. neutrophils

42. a. lymphocytes   b. monocytes

43. neutrophils

44. bone morrow

45. bone morrow and some lymph tissue

46. fragments

47. aid in blood clotting

48. ribs, skull, humerus, hip bones, vertebrae

49. pluripotent stem cells

50. hematopoietic growth factors (HGFs)

51. a. erythropoietin
   b. colony-stimulating factor (CSF)
   c. interleukins

52. a. 4.5 to 5.5 million/mm³
   b. 7000 to 10,000/mm³
   c. 250,000/mm³
   d. 42 to 45 percent
   e. 14 to 16 gm/dl

53. diffusion, mediated transport

54. 5 percent

55. See Fig. 14.13, p. 409. The four chambers are the right atrium, right ventricle, left atrium, and left ventricle.

56. a. right ventricle
   b. left atrium
   c. left ventricle

57. arteries

58. veins

59. aorta, arteries, arterioles, capillaries, venules, veins

60. superior vena cava

61. inferior vena cava, right atrium

62. low

63. high

64. oxygenated

65. oxygenated

66. lungs

67. entire systemic circulation except for the lungs

68. $F = \Delta P/R$, where F = flow (L/min), P = pressure difference (mmHg), and R = resistance

69. Flow rate is directly proportional to the pressure difference and inversely proportional to the resistance to flow.

70. a. resistance
     b. viscosity
     c. length of vessel (or tube)
     d. radius of vessel (or tube)

71. increase, decrease

72. radius, or r^4

73. 16

74. pericardium

75. myocardium

76. endothelium

77. See Fig. 14.13, p. 409.

78. a. tricuspid
     b. mitral
     c. pulmonary
     d. aortic

79. AV, chordae tendinae

80.
Cardiac muscle	Skeletal muscle	Smooth muscle
straited	straited	nonstraited or smooth
involuntary	voluntary	involuntary

81. electrical conducting system

82. atrial natriuretic factor (ANF)

83. a. sympathetic
     b. parasympathetic
     c. norepinephrine
     d. achetylcholine
     e. adrenergic (beta)
     f. cholinergic (muscarinic)

84. coronary

85. A: resting membrane potential
     B: depolarization
     C: plateau
     D: repolarization

86. B: increased; P_{Na^+} due to opening of voltage-sensitive Na^+ channels
     C: increased; $P_{Ca^{2+}}$ due to opening of voltage-sensitive Ca^{2+} channels
     D: increased; P_{K^+}, slow Ca^{2+} channels close and K^+ channels reopen

87. See Fig. 14-17, page 413.

88. pacemaker potential (local) (generator), action potential

89. automaticity (or spontaneous excitability)

90. 72

91. a. increase   b. decrease   c. increase

92. SA nodal

93. See Fig. 14-18, page 414.

94. AV node

95. Fig. 14-21A, page 415, shows five sequential heartbeats.

96. atrial depolarization

97. ventricular depolarization

98. ventricular repolarization

99. See Fig. 14-20, page 415.

100. electrical

101. a. Action potential moves into cardiac muscle cells via the T tubules.
    b. Action potential opens voltage-sensitive Ca^{2+} channels in the T-tubule membranes.
    c. The increased cytosol Ca^{2+} acts on the adjacent sarcoplasmic reticulum to increase the amount of Ca^{2+} released from the sarcoplasmic reticulum.
    d. Ca^{2+} binds to the troponin to initiate the events leading to muscle contraction.

102. the period of time during and following an action potential during which an excitable membrane cannot be reexcited

103.

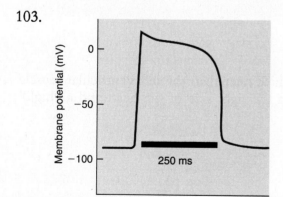

104. Due to the long refractory period, a second action potential cannot be elicited "fast enough" to cause tetanization.

105. systole, diastole

106. systole

107. diastole

108. A: isovolumetric ventricular contraction
     B: ventricular ejection
     C: isovolumetric ventricular relaxation
     D: ventricular filling

109. systole: isovolumetric ventricular contraction (A) and ventricular ejection (B)
     diastole: isovolumetric ventricular relaxation (C) and ventricular filling (D)

110. stroke volume

111. 80 percent

112. pulmonic and aortic, tricuspid and mitral

113. end diastolic volume, 135

114. AV, semilunar

115. end systolic volume, 65

116. stroke volume (135 ml − 65 ml = 70 ml)

117. decrease, no change

118. decrease

119. a. 24   b. 8   c. 120   d. 80

120. 70 ml/beat

121. 70 ml/beat

122. The right ventricular muscle wall is much thinner than the left ventricular muscle wall, correlating with a "low" pressure in the right side of the heart and a "high" pressure in the left side of the heart.

123. closure of the AV valves

124. closure of the semilunar valves

125. CO is the amount of blood pumped by one ventricle per minute (L/min).

126. SV

127. 5, 70

128. 9.6 L/min (80 beats/min × 120 ml/beat = 9.6 L/min)

129. without

130. decreases

131. increases

132. parasympathetic

133. c

134. b

135. SV is the volume of blood ejected per beat (approximately 70 ml/beat).

136. a. Change in end diastolic volume (EDV) (Starling's law of the heart)
     b. Change in sympathetic firing to the heart muscle

137. This law states that the greater the ventricular end diastolic volume (or venous return), the greater the force of contraction (or stroke volume).

138. norepinephrine, adrenergic, increase

139. SV, 50 to 67 percent

140. increases

141. $C = \Delta V/\Delta P$

142. veins

143. Compliance is decreased.

144. 125 mmHg

145. 75 mmHg

146. DP

147. 50 mmHg

148. a. stroke volume (SV)   b. arterial compliance

149. increase

150. decrease

151. increase

152. PP

153. 176.6 mmHg (MAP = 160 + 1/3(70))

154. Inflate the cuff around the brachial region of the arm and listen with a stethoscope for the first audible sound (systolic BP) and for the disappearance of the sounds (diastolic BP).

155. R organ

156. myogenic

157. a. local control mechanisms   b. extrinsic (neural) control mechanisms

158. vasodilation, hyperemia

159. vasodilation

160. increase

161. norepinephrine, alpha (α) adrenergic

162. a. VC   c. VC   e. VC
     b. VD   d. VC   f. VD

163. a. VD   b. VD   c. VC

164. approximately 5 percent

165. exchange of nutrients,
     exchange of metabolic end products,
     exchange of gases

166. equal to, less than

167. a. single cell layer of endothelial cells
     b. transitional vessels between arterioles and capillaries
     c. ring of smooth muscle between arterioles and capillaries or metarterioles and capillaries

168. Velocity of blood flow is slowest in the capillaries because they have the greatest total cross-sectional area, and fastest in the aorta and vena cava because they have the smallest total cross-sectional area.

169. a. diffusion (nutrients, O_2, metabolic end products)
     b. vesicle transport
     c. bulk flow (protein-free plasma)

170. interstitial, cells

171. interstitial fluid, plasma

172. concentration

173. The movement of fluid across the capillary wall depends on (1) capillary hydrostatic pressure, (2) interstitial hydrostatic pressure, (3) plasma protein concentration, and (4) interstitial fluid protein concentration. The balance in these forces determines whether filtration (net movement of fluid out of the capillary) or absorption (net movement of fluid into the capillary) will occur.

174. Veins are low-resistance conduits because their pressure is 5 to 10 mmHg, offering little resistance to flow.

175. a.   approx. 100 mmHg
     b.   approx. 35 to 25 mmHg
     c.   approx. 10 to 5 mmHg

176. Veins have valves to prevent "backflow" of the low-pressure venous blood.

177. a. V   b. A   c. V

178. sympathetic

179. a. venoconstriction   b. skeletal-muscle pump   d. respiratory pump

180. Any change in venous return will change cardiac output, primarily through Starling's law of the heart. (Increased venous return leads to an increase in cardiac output.)

181. lymph nodes, lymph vessels, lymph

182. veins in the lower neck

183. true

184. blood capillaries

185. edema

186. smooth

187. skeletal muscle, respiratory

188.   a. MAP

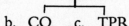

                              b. CO   c. TPR

     a. MAP, mean arterial pressure
     b. CO, cardiac output
     c. TPR, total peripheral resistance

189. a. carotid sinus   b. aortic arch

190.

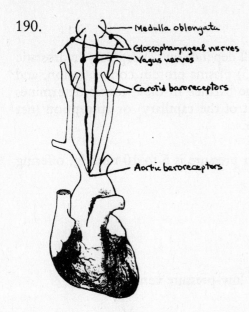

Medulla oblongata
Glossopharyngeal nerves
Vagus nerves
Carotid baroreceptors
Aortic baroreceptors

191. See glossopharyngeal and vagus above.

192. increases

193.

Arterial baroreceptors ➡ Medullary cardiovascular center

Parasympathetic ➡ Heart

Sympathetic ➡ Heart
Arterioles
Veins

194.

⬆ Parasympathetic firing

⬆MAP➡ ⬆ Baroreceptor firing ➡ Medulla — ⬇ CO and ⬇ TPR and ⬇ MAP

⬇ Sympathetic firing

⬇ Parasympathetic firing

⬇MAP➡ ⬇ Baroreceptor firing ➡ Medulla — ⬆ CO and ⬆ TPR and ⬆ MAP

⬆ Sympathetic firing

195. short

196. blood volume

197. decrease, decrease

198. increase, increase

199. a. I   c. I   e. I
    b. I   d. I   f. I to return
                                                                                 to normal

200. nearly normal because of the movement of interstitial fluid into the capillaries

201. decrease

202. There is an increase in capillary pressure in the feet due to gravity, which leads to increased filtration of fluid out of the capillaries into the interstitial fluid spaces (i.e., an increase in capillary hydrostatic pressure).

203. There is minimal skeletal-muscle contraction to aid in venous return. The decreased venous return leads to a decrease in BP, which leads to fainting.

204. a. I   c. I   e. D
    b. I   d. D   f. I
                                                                                g. I

205. Chronically elevated systemic arterial pressure, usually greater than 140/90 mmHg.

206. In primary hypertension, the cause is unknown. In renal hypertension, there is a severe disorder associated with the kidneys leading to hypertension.

207. excessive salt intake, obesity, cigarette smoking, stress, lack of exercise

208. diuretics, beta receptor blockers, Ca^{2+} channel blockers, angiotensin II blockers, sympathetic nervous system inhibitors

209. See Fig. 14-71, page 468.

210. increases, decreases

211. a. Systemic edema occurs from elevated venous pressure (due to increased extracellular volume), causing increased capillary pressure and increased capillary filtration into the interstitial spaces, hence edema.
    b. Pulmonary edema occurs from a decrease in left ventricular pumping ability, leading to an imbalance in the output of the right and left ventricles. Hence the greater output from the right ventricle than from the left ventricle results in increased fluid in the pulmonary capillaries, leading to increased filtration and pulmonary edema.

212. a. decreases fluid volume
    b. decreases fluid volume
    c. decreases TPR and afterload (MAP)

213. cardiac muscle

214. a. chest pain associated with myocardial ischemia
   b. heart muscle damage or death due to decreased coronary flow
   c. hardening of the arteries
   d. a form of arteriosclerosis due to plaque formation from increased smooth-muscle cells, cholesterol, or related substances

215. a. dilates coronary arteries and systemic arterioles, resulting in a decrease in TPR and a decrease in the workload on the heart
   b. decreases the workload on the heart and decreases the O_2 demand
   c. decreases the workload on the heart and causes vasodilation
   d. prevents life-threatening blood clots from developing

216. a. localized brain damage due to an occluded or ruptured cerebral blood vessel
   b. a wandering blood clot that may lodge "downstream" and occlude a smaller vessel

CHAPTER
15
RESPIRATION

ORGANIZATION OF THE RESPIRATORY SYSTEM

1. Diagram the human respiratory system.

2. Movement of air from the environment through the airways into the alveoli during breathing is _____ .

3. Movement of air from the alveoli through the airway into the environment is _____ .

The Airways

4. The pathway of air through the upper airways (in order) is:

5. The larynx opens into the _____ which branches into _____ bronchi, one of which enters each lung.

6. The trachea and bronchi, composed of smooth muscle, have C-shaped rings composed of _____ (incomplete posteriorly). These rings provide _____ to the airways.

7. The bronchi further divide into _____ which have terminal bronchioles from which grapelike clusters of _____ arise.

Review Fig. 15-2, page 476, and Fig. 5-3, page 477.

8. The two zones of the airways beyond the larynx are:

   a.

   b.

9. Which zone has no alveoli present and has no gas exchange with the blood?

10. Which zone contains alveoli and has gas exchange occurring with the blood?

11. What are the functions of the cilia, mucus, watery fluid, and macrophages in the airways?

12. How does the genetic disease cystic fibrosis affect lung function?

Site of Gas Exchange: The Alveoli

13. Describe the alveolar-capillary membrane.

Review Fig. 15-4 A and B, page 478.

14. The total surface area of the alveoli in contact with the pulmonary capillaries is (*greater than, less than, approximately equal to*) the size of a tennis court.

15. The thickness of this alveolar capillary membrane is (*greater than, less than, approximately equal to*) the diameter of an erythrocyte.

16. What is the most important function that occurs at this alveolar-capillary membrane?

17. Differentiate between type I and type II alveolar cells.

Relation of the Lungs to the Thoracic (Chest) Wall

18. Define the following:

    a. Diaphragm:

    b. Intercostal muscles:

    c. Visceral pleura:

    d. Parietal pleura:

    e. Intrapleural fluid:

Pulmonary Pressure

19. The volume of air in the lungs at the end of an unforced expiration when no significant respiratory muscle contraction is occurring is called _____.

20. Describe the following:
    a. Atmospheric pressure (P_{atm}):

    b. Alveolar pressure (P_{alv}):

    c. Intrapleural pressure (P_{ip}):

    d. Transpulmonary pressure (P_{tp}):

21. When a person suffers a stab wound through the chest wall, the lung volume decreases and the chest wall expands outward. Explain why this happens. Incorporate the above pressures into your answer.

VENTILATION AND LUNG MECHANICS

Review Fig. 15-7.

22. Air, like blood, always moves (*up, down*) its pressure gradient.

23. $F_{air} = \dfrac{?}{R}$

24. Since atmospheric pressure remains relatively constant, for air to move in and out of the lungs, the pressure in the _____ must be less than atmospheric pressure during inspiration and greater than atmospheric pressure during expiration.

25. Boyle's law helps explain how air can move into and out of the lungs. State this law.

Review Fig. 15-9, page 481.

Inspiration

26. The major skeletal muscles involved in inspiration are the _____ and the _____.

27. Label the alveolar pressure, intrapleural pressure, and transpulmonary pressure lines on the graph on the right.

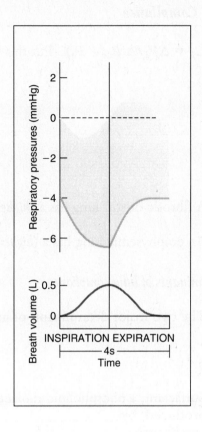

28. Explain why air moves into the alveoli during inspiration.

Expiration

29. Explain why air moves out of the alveoli during expiration.

30. At rest, expiration is (*active, passive*) and does not require active muscle contraction. During exercise, expiration may be (*active, passive*). The muscles that actively contract to decrease thoracic dimensions include the _____ and _____ muscles.

31. How do you forcefully exhale to "blow up" a balloon, sing, or play a tuba?

Lung Compliance

32. $C_L = \Delta V_L / \Delta(P_{alv} - P_{ip})$. Put this formula for lung compliance into words.

33. A fibrotic or stiff lung has a (*higher, lower*) compliance than normal.

34. An emphysemic lung has a (*higher, lower*) compliance than normal.

Determinants of lung compliance

35. The two major determinants of lung compliance are:
    a.
    b.

36. Surfactant, a phospholipid molecule, is a surface tension-(*reducing, increasing*) substance produced by _____ alveolar cells that will (*increase, decrease*) lung compliance.

37. In newborns who have respiratory distress syndrome (RDS), compliance is greatly (*increased, decreased*) because of the absence of _____ .

Airway Resistance

38. The major factor that determines airway resistance to air flow is _____ .

39. In an asthmatic individual, there is a(n) (*increase, decrease*) in airway resistance when _____ muscle contracts in response to an underlying inflammation or hypersensitivity to various agents.

40. In an emphysemic individual, there is a(n) (*increase, decrease*) in lung compliance due to the destruction of the elastic tissue of the lung.

41. In chronic bronchitis, with excess mucus production in the bronchi and chronic inflammation in the small airways, the (*outflow, inflow*) of air is primarily obstructed. Why?

Lung Volumes and Capacities

42. Fill in the blanks:

Identify   Volume
           (ml)

A: ____ ____
B: ____ ____
C: ____ ____
D: ____ ____
E: ____ ____
F: ____ ____
G: ____ ____
H: ____ ____

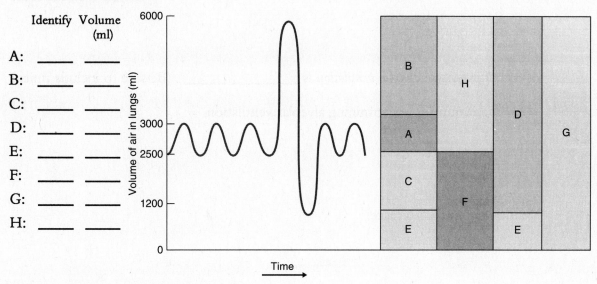

43. Complete the following formulas:

    a. TLC = VC + _____

    b. FRC = RV + _____

    c. VC = ERV + ____ + ____

44. Normal individuals can forcefully exhale in 1 s (FEV_1) _____percent of their forced vital capacity (FVC).

45. People with *obstructive disorders* (emphysema, chronic bronchitis) have a(n) (*increase, decrease*) in FEV_1. Why?

46. People with *restrictive disorders* (fibrosis) who have normal airway resistance but stiff lungs, pleura, or chest wall, have a(n) (*increase, decrease, normal*) FEV_1. Why?

Alveolar Ventilation

47. The value for normal *minute ventilation* is _____ . (Be sure to include units.)

48. Write the formula for determining minute ventilation.

49. A value for normal *alveolar ventilation* is _____ . (Be sure to include units.)

50. Write the formula for determining alveolar ventilation.

51. Define anatomic dead space:

52. An effective way of significantly increasing alveolar ventilation is by increasing the (*rate, depth*) of respiration.

53. Define alveolar dead space:

54. Physiologic dead space consists of _____ and _____ .

EXCHANGE OF GASES IN ALVEOLI AND TISSUES

55. The formula for determining respiratory quotient (RQ) is _____ .

56. A normal value for RQ for an individual on a mixed diet is _____ .

Partial Pressures of Gases

57. Define partial pressure of a gas:

58. Assuming an atmospheric pressure of 760 mmHg, what are the partial pressures for the following atmospheric gases?

a. P_{O_2} = _____ mmHg

b. P_{CO_2} = _____ mmHg

c. P_{N_2} = _____ mmHg

Diffusion of gases in liquids

59. Gas molecules diffuse between liquid and gas phases or within liquid or gas phases based on the fact that gas molecules diffuse from an area of (*higher, lower*) concentration to an area of (*higher, lower*) concentration.

Alveolar Gas Pressures

60. Fill in the blanks:

Atmospheric gases	Alveolar gases	Arterial gases
a. P_{atm,O_2} ____ mmHg	c. P_{alv,O_2} ____ mmHg	e. Pa_{O_2} ____ mmHg
b. P_{atm,CO_2} ____ mmHg	d. P_{alv,CO_2} ____ mmHg	f. Pa_{CO_2} ____ mmHg

61. If alveolar ventilation is reduced in an individual with normal cellular O_2 utilization and CO_2 production, the alveolar P_{O_2} will (*increase, decrease*) and the alveolar P_{CO_2} will (*increase, decrease*).

62. If the ratio of O_2 consumption to alveolar ventilation increases, the alveolar P_{O_2} will (*increase, decrease*).

63. If the ratio of CO_2 production to alveolar ventilation increases, the alveolar P_{CO_2} will (*increase, decrease*).

64. An increase in the ratio of CO_2 production to alveolar ventilation occurs during (*hypoventilation, hyperventilation*).

Alveolar-Blood Gas Exchange

65. Fill in the blanks:

Systemic arterial blood	Systemic venous blood	Pulmonary arterial blood	Pulmonary venous blood
a. P_{O_2} ____	c. P_{O_2} ____	e. P_{O_2} ____	g. P_{O_2} ____
b. P_{CO_2} ____	d. P_{CO_2} ____	f. P_{CO_2} ____	h. P_{CO_2} ____

66. Fill in the blanks for the P_{gas} values:

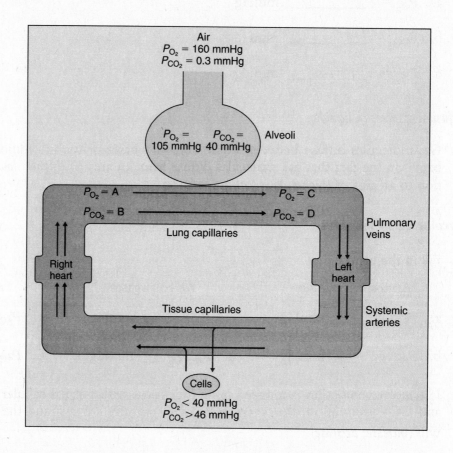

67. In the figure above, indicate with an arrow the direction that O_2 and CO_2 move across the alveolar-capillary membrane.

68. Alveolar gas pressures are determined by:

    a.

    b.

    c.

69. Diffusion of gases across the alveolar-capillary membrane may be impaired by:

    a.

    b.

    c.

Matching of Ventilation and Blood Flow in Alveoli

70. Normally, alveolar ventilation (V_{alv}) and pulmonary capillary perfusion (Q_c) are matched. ($V_{alv}/Q_c = 4.2$ L/min/5.0 L/min). In disease states such as emphysema where alveolar ventilation is impaired, what happens to the gas exchange as reflected in the P_{alv,O_2} and the Pa_{CO_2}?

71. If the alveolar P_{O_2} is low because of decreased alveolar ventilation, the low P_{O_2} causes (*vasoconstriction, vasodilation*) of the small pulmonary vessels supplying blood to these alveoli. Why is this advantageous?

Gas Exchange in the Tissues

72. Fill in the blanks:

P_{O_2} gradient		P_{CO_2} gradient	
a. alveoli (_____)		d. cells (_____)	
↓		↓	
b. _____(_____)		e. _____(_____)	
↓		↓	
c. _____(_____)		f. _____(_____)	

TRANSPORT OF OXYGEN IN BLOOD

73. Oxygen is carried in blood in two forms:
    a.
    b.

74. What percentage of oxygen is carried in each form?

75. Each hemoglobin molecule can bind with _____ molecules of oxygen.

76. Define percent saturation of hemoglobin with oxygen:

77. What factors determine the percent hemoglobin saturation?

    a.

    b.

78. Differentiate between O_2 *content* and *percent saturation of hemoglobin with* O_2.

79. At a P_{O_2} of 100 mmHg, the arterial O_2 content = _____. (Be sure to include units.)

80. At a P_{O_2} of 100 mmHg, the arterial O_2 saturation of hemoglobin with O_2 = _____. (Be sure to include units.)

Effect of P_{O_2} on Hemoglobin Saturation

81. Draw an O_2-hemoglobin dissociation curve. Be sure to label the X and Y axes.

82. The steep portion of this curve lies between P_{O_2} values of _____, and the plateau occurs between P_{O_2} values of _____.

83. The P_{O_2} of blood is a result of the (*dissolved oxygen, oxygen combined with hemoglobin*).

84. The O_2 available for direct gas exchange from the blood to the cells is the (*dissolved oxygen, oxygen combined with hemoglobin*).

Review Fig. 15-20, page 495.

Effects of Blood P_{CO_2}, H⁺ Concentration, Temperature, and DPG Concentration on Hemoglobin Saturation

85. An *increase* in P_{CO_2}, H⁺ concentration, temperature, or 2,3-DPG causes the O_2-hemoglobin dissociation curve to shift to the (*right, left*).

86. A right curve shift indicates that hemoglobin has a (*greater, lesser*) affinity for O_2.

87. A right curve shift favors the (*loading, unloading*) of O_2 from the hemoglobin molecule. During severe exercise there is a (*right, left*) curve shift in the O_2-hemoglobin dissociation curve. Why?

88. During glycolysis, 2,3-DPG is produced in erythrocytes. An increase in the 2,3-DPG favors (*loading, unloading*) of O_2 for the hemoglobin.

TRANSPORT OF CARBON DIOXIDE IN BLOOD

89. Why is the CO_2 content greater than the O_2 content in blood?

90. CO_2 is transported in blood in three ways:
    a.
    b.
    c.

91. Complete this equation:

$$CO_2 + H_2O \xrightleftharpoons{A} H_2CO_3 \rightleftharpoons \underline{\qquad} + \underline{\qquad}$$

92. The enzyme that catalyzes the above reaction at point A is _____.

93. The chloride shift is the process by which ____ions from inside the erythrocytes move out to the plasma in exchange for _____ ions.

TRANSPORT OF HYDROGEN IONS BETWEEN TISSUES AND LUNGS

94. Complete the following equation:

$$HbO_2 + H^+ \rightleftharpoons \underline{\hspace{1cm}} + \underline{\hspace{1cm}}$$

95. Systemic arterial blood pH is (*greater than, less than*) venous blood pH. Why?

96. An increase in arterial P_{CO_2} will (*increase, decrease*) arterial H^+ concentration and (*increase, decrease*) arterial pH. This increase in P_{CO_2} is indicative of a respiratory (*acidosis, alkalosis*).

97. Hyperventilation will (*increase, decrease*) arterial P_{CO_2}, (*increase, decrease*) arterial H^+ concentration, and (*increase, decrease*) arterial pH. This may lead to a respiratory (*acidosis, alkalosis*).

CONTROL OF RESPIRATION

Neural Control of Rhythmic Breathing

98. The central integrating center for control of motor output to the skeletal muscles involved in respiration is located in the _____ .

99. Inspiratory and expiratory neurons have inherent rhythmicity such that when the inspiratory neurons fire, _____ occurs, and when these neurons are at rest, _____ occurs.

Control of Ventilation by P_{O_2}, P_{CO_2} and H^+ Concentration

100. The two types of chemoreceptors that send afferent input into the medullary respiratory center are:

    a.

    b.

101. Indicate where each of these chemoreceptors is located, the most potent stimulus to respiration for each, and what changes in alveolar ventilation are brought about by this stimulus.

	Location	Stimulus	Change in alveolar ventilation
a. Central			
b. Peripheral			

102. The chemoreceptors most sensitive to *small* changes in P_{CO_2} are the _____ chemoreceptors.

103. In *metabolic* acidosis, the _____ chemoreceptors are stimulated by an increase in _____. This reflex input into the medullary respiratory center will (*increase, decrease*) alveolar ventilation.

104. How do the following parameters change during *metabolic alkalosis*?

a. Arterial pH:

b. Arterial H^+ concentration:

c. Alveolar ventilation:

105. Indicate whether an increase or decrease in the following parameters will *increase* alveolar ventilation.

a. P_{O_2}:

b. P_{CO_2}:

c. H^+ concentration:

Control of Ventilation During Exercise

106. Several factors that increase alveolar ventilation during exercise are:

Other Ventilatory Responses

107. Protective reflexes of the respiratory system include:

108. Control of respiration is primarily under (*voluntary, involuntary*) control. Breath holding and hyperventilation are examples of _____ control of breathing.

109. Indicate the effects of breath holding and hyperventilation on arterial P_{O_2} and P_{CO_2}.

	Arterial P_{O_2}	Arterial P_{CO_2}
a. Breath holding	a.	c.
b. Hyperventilation	b.	d.

HYPOXIA

110. Define hypoxia:

111. List the various categories of hypoxia.
    a.
    b.
    c.
    d.

Review Table 15-11, page 509.

Acclimatization to High Altitude

112. As altitude increases, atmospheric pressure (*increases, decreases*)

113. If the atmospheric pressure on the top of the mountain you are living on is 375 mmHg, calculate the following parameters:
    a. P_{O_2} = _____   b. P_{CO_2} = _____   c. P_{N_2} = _____
    Show your work:

114. If you live on the top of this mountain for 1 year, will your hematocrit change? Why?

Review the SUMMARY, REVIEW QUESTIONS, and THOUGHT QUESTIONS at the end of this chapter in your textbook.

CHAPTER 15 ANSWER KEY

1. See Fig. 15-1, page 475.

2. inspiration

3. expiration

4. nose or mouth to pharynx to larynx

5. trachea, two

6. cartilage, support

7. bronchioles, alveoli

8. a. conducting zone
   b. respiratory zone

9. conducting zone

10. respiratory zone

11. These keep the lungs clear of particulate matter and bacteria, acting like a mucus escalator to move particulate matter up to pharynx so it can be swallowed.

12. There is impaired chloride secretion that impairs the secretion of watery fluid into airways; thus the secretions become thick (dehydrated).

13. The alveolar-capillary membrane consists of the alveolar membrane in close proximity to the pulmonary capillary membrane with a very thin space between them. These single-cell-thick membranes are the site of gas exchange.

14. approximately equal to

15. less than; alveolar membrane, 0.2 μm; erythrocyte diameter, 7 μm

16. gas exchange

17. Type I cells line the alveoli. Type II cells produce surfactant, a surface tension-reducing agent. These specialized cells are fewer in number than type I cells.

18. a. skeletal muscle that separates the thoracic cavity from the abdominal cavity; an important muscle in respiration
    b. skeletal muscle located between the ribs involved in respiration
    c. pleural membrane that adheres to the surface of the lungs
    d. pleural membrane that adheres to the thoracic cage wall
    e. fluid present between the visceral and parietal pleura

19. FRC

20. a. pressure of atmosphere air; at sea level, P_{atm} = 760 mmHg
    b. pressure in alveoli (+4 to –4 mmHg with respect to atmospheric pressure during expiration and inspiration, respectively
    c. pressure in the intrapleural space; always negative with respect to atmospheric pressure
    d. alveolar pressure – intrapleural pressure ($P_{alv} - P_{IP}$)

21. The stab wound allows atmospheric air to enter into the intrapleural space, removing this negative (subatmospheric) pressure, which in turn allows the lung to "recoil" or decrease in size and the chest wall to expand outward. Also the transpulmonary pressure is altered.

22. down

23. $P_{atm} - P_{alv}$

24. alveoli

25. Boyle's law states that the pressure of a gas increases when the volume in which it is contained decreases, and vice versa. (There is an inverse relationship between volume and pressure.)

26. diaphragm, intercostal muscles

27. See Fig. 15-11, page 482.

28. Air moves into the alveoli during inspiration because P_{alv} is less than atmospheric pressure (P_{atm}). [The diaphragm and intercostal muscles contract; the lung and chest wall expand; P_{alv} is less than P_{atm}; air flows in (inspiration).]

29. Air moves out of the alveoli during expiration because P_{alv} is greater than P_{atm}. [The diaphragm and intercostal muscles relax; the lungs and chest wall return to their original size; P_{alv} is greater than P_{atm}; air flows out (expiration).]

30. passive, active, internal intercostals, abdominal

31. Forceful exhalation is due to abdominal muscle compression which forces the diaphragm "upward" to increase P_{alv} and force air out. Internal intercostal muscles also assist somewhat.

32. The compliance of the lung (C_L) is represented by the ratio of the change in lung volume (ΔLv) for each unit of change in transpulmonary pressure [$\Delta(P_{alv} - P_{ip})$].

33. lower

34. higher

35. a. stretchability of the lung tissue
    b. surface tension at the air-water interface

36. reducing, type II, increase

37. decreased, surfactant

38. airway diameter

39. increase, bronchial smooth

40. increase

41. Outflow is affected primarily because inspiration is *active* but expiration, at rest, is *passive*.

42.
a: TV	500	d: VC	5000	g: TLC	6000
b: IRV	3000	e: RV	1000	h: IC	3500
c: ERV	1500	f: FRC	2500		

43. a. RV   b. ERV   c. TV, IRV

44. 80 percent

45. decrease. The narrowed airways from the obstructive disorder make forced expiration difficult.

46. normal. The restrictive disorder primarily restricts input (inhalation) and does not affect exhalation.

47. approx. 5 to 6 L/min

48. V_{min} = TV $\times f$ (500 ml/breath $\times$ 10 to 12 breaths/min), where TV = tidal volume and f = frequency or rate of breathing

49. approx. 3.5 to 4.5 L/min

50. V_{alv} = (TV – DS) $\times f$ (500 ml/beat – 150 ml/beat) $\times$ (10 to 12 breaths/min)

51. space occupied by air which is present in the airways but not in the alveoli and therefore does not participate in gas exchange.

52. depth

53. volume of air in which the alveoli are not ventilated or the capillaries to those alveoli are not perfused

54. anatomic dead space, alveolar, dead space

55. CO_2 produced/O_2 consumed

56. 0.8

57. pressure that gas alone exerts in a mixture of gases

58. a. 159.6 (0.21 × 760 mmHg)
    b. 0.03 (0.0004 × 760 mmHg)
    c. 600.4 (0.79 × 760 mmHg)

59. higher, lower

60. a. approx. 160   c. approx. 105   e. approx. 100
    b. approx. 0.3   d. approx. 40   f. approx. 40

61. decrease, increase

62. decrease

63. increase

64. hypoventilation

65. a. 100   d. 46   g. 100
    b. 40   e. 40   h. 40
    c. 40   f. 46

66. a. 40   c. 100
    b. 46   d. 40

67. See Fig. 15-17, page 490.

68. a. atmospheric P_{O_2} (P_{atm,O_2})
    b. cellular O_2 consumption and CO_2 production
    c. alveolar ventilation

69. a. decreased surface area available for gas exchange
    b. increased thickness of the alveolar-capillary membrane
    c. decrease in pressure gradient for the gases

70. There would be a decrease in $P_{a_{O_2}}$ and no change in $P_{a_{CO_2}}$ unless the inequality is very severe.

71. vasoconstriction. This will reduce the blood flow to the poorly ventilated areas and shunt the blood to the well-ventilated areas.

72. a. alveoli (105 mmHg)   d. cells (46 mmHg)
    ↓   ↓
    b. blood (100 mmHg)   e. blood (46 mmHg)
    ↓   ↓
    c. cells (approx. 20 mmHg)   f. alveoli (40 mmHg)

73. a. dissolved

b. combined reversibly with hemoglobin

74. Approx. 3 percent is dissolved in plasma, and approx. 97 percent is combined with hemoglobin.

75. four

76. (amount of O_2 combined with hemoglobin/maximum possible amount) $\times 100$

77. a. plasma P_{O_2}
    b. hemoglobin content

78. O_2 content is milliliters of O_2/100 ml of blood. Percent saturation of hemoglobin with O_2 is the *percentage* of hemoglobin saturated with O_2.

79. 20 ml/100 ml blood

80. 97 percent

81. See Fig. 15-20, page 495.

82. 10 and 60 mmHg, 70 to 100 mmHg

83. dissolved oxygen

84. dissolved oxygen

85. right

86. lesser

87. unloading, right. During severe exercise, there are increases in CO_2, lactic acid, H^+, temperature, 2,3-DPG—all of which cause a right curve shift.

88. unloading

89. CO_2 content = 46 to 52 volume % (46 to 52 ml/100 ml blood)
    O_2 content = 15 to 20 vol % (15 to 20 ml/100 ml blood)
    CO_2 is much more soluble in water than is oxygen.

90. a. dissolved (approx. 10 percent)
    b. carbamino form (approx. 30 percent)
    c. as bicarbonate ion (HCO_3^-) (approx. 60 percent)

91. H^+, HCO_3^-

92. carbonic anhydrase

93. HCO_3^-, C^-

94. HbH, O_2

95. greater than. There is more CO_2 in venous blood which generates H^+ by the reaction $CO_2 + H_2O \rightleftharpoons H_2CO_3 \rightleftharpoons H^+ + HCO_3^-$.

96. increase, decrease, acidosis

97. decrease, decrease, increase, alkalosis

98. medulla oblongata

99. inspiration, expiration

100. a. central chemoreceptors
    b. peripheral chemoreceptors

101. a. medulla   ↑ or ↓ in P_{CO_2} ↑ or ↓ in V_{alv}

    b. carotid and
       aortic bodies   ↑ P_{CO_2} ↑ V_{alv}
                        ↑ H^+ ↑ V_{alv}
                        ↓ P_{O_2} below 60 mmHg   ↑ V_{alv}

102. central

103. peripheral, H^+, increase

104. a. increases   b. decreases   c. decreases

105. a. decrease   b. increase   c. increase

106. increased afferent input from joint and muscle receptors, increased body temperature, increased circulating epinephrine and norepinephrine, learned response

107. cough, sneeze, noxious agents

108. involuntary, voluntary

109. a. decreases   c. increases
    b. increases   d. decreases

110. a deficiency of oxygen at the tissue level

111. a. hypoxic hypoxia (hypoxemia)   c. ischemic hypoxia
    b. anemic hypoxia   d. histotoxic hypoxia

113. a. 78.75   b. 0.15   c. 296.25 mmHg

P_{O_2} $= 0.21 \times 375 = 78.75$
PC_{O_2} $= 0.0004 \times 375 = 0.15$
P_{N_2} $= 0.79 \times 375 = 296.25$

114. Yes, the hematocrit will *increase* due to the low O_2, which stimulates increased erythropoietin from the kidney, which in turn increases erythropoiesis in the bone marrow.

CHAPTER
16
THE KIDNEYS AND REGULATION
OF WATER AND INORGANIC IONS

Section A. Basic Principles of Renal Physiology

FUNCTIONS OF THE KIDNEY

1. List at least five major functions of the kidneys:

   a.

   b.

   c.

   d.

   e.

STRUCTURE OF THE KIDNEYS AND URINARY SYSTEM

2. Diagram the gross anatomy of the renal system. Label the kidneys, ureters, urinary bladder, and urethra.

3. Diagram a coronal section of the kidney. Label the pyramids, renal cortex, renal medulla, and renal pelvis.

4. Diagram the anatomy of the nephron. Label the afferent arteriole, efferent arteriole, peritubular capillaries, vasa recta, glomerulus, Bowman's capsule, proximal tubule, loop of Henle (ascending limb and descending limb) distal tubule, collecting duct.

5. Differentiate between cortical and juxtamedullary nephrons.

6. The juxtaglomerular apparatus (JGA) is composed of the _____ and the _____ .

7. Draw the JGA.

BASIC RENAL PROCESSES

8. The three processes that occur in the nephron during urine formation are:

    a.

    b.

    c.

9. The glomerular filtrate is plasma minus _____.

10. The membranes that filtrate crosses from the glomerular capillaries to Bowman's capsule are (in order):

    a.

    b.

    c.

11. Differentiate between tubular reabsorption and tubular secretion.

12. The amount of any substance *excreted* in the urine is equal to the amount filtered plus the amount (*secreted*, *reabsorbed*) minus the amount (*secreted*, *reabsorbed*).

13. Approximately _____ percent of the plasma entering the glomerulus is filtered.

Glomerular Filtration

14. Describe the contents of glomerular filtrate.

Forces involved in filtration

15. List the forces involved in glomerular filtration.

    a.

    b.

    c.

16. Glomerular capillary hydrostatic pressure is normally about _____ mmHg.

17. Net glomerular filtration pressure is normally about _____ mmHg.

Rate of glomerular filtration

18. In a 70-kg person (_____ lb) the normal glomerular filtration rate is _____ ml/min (_____ L/day).

19. The kidneys receive approx. _____ percent of the cardiac output.

20. Determine how many times your plasma is filtered each day. Show your work.

21. Why is it more correct to say "plasma is filtered" than "blood is filtered"?

22. Define filtered load.

23. Determine the filtered load for a substance with a plasma concentration of 76 mg/100 ml of blood. Show your work.

24. If the amount of the above substance excreted into the urine is 24 g/day, is this substance secreted or reabsorbed? _____ Why?

Tubular Reabsorption

Review Table 16-2, page 524.

25. Define tubular reabsorption.

26. Draw a kidney tubule and a peritubular capillary. Use an arrow to show the direction of movement of substances in tubular reabsorption.

27. Normally, _____ is completely reabsorbed from the proximal tubules.

28. Water and inorganic ions (*are, are not*) completely reabsorbed from the proximal tubules.

29. In contrast to glomerular filtration which occurs by bulk flow, reabsorption of substances from the tubular lumen into the interstitial fluid is by _____ and _____.

30. Movement of reabsorbed substances from the interstitial fluid into the peritubular capillaries is by _____ and _____.

T_m-limited transport mechanisms

31. Define T_m.

32. Explain why an individual with a plasma glucose of 375 mg/100 ml blood will have glucose in the urine. (Normal glucose is approx. 100 mg/100 ml blood, and the T_m for glucose is 375 mg/min.) *Hint:* The filtered load for glucose equals plasma glucose × GFR.

Reabsorption by diffusion

33. A compound in which 50 percent of the filtered load is reabsorbed from the tubule by diffusion is _____. The reabsorption of this compound is a passive process dependent on the reabsorption of water. Explain.

Tubular Secretion

34. Define tubular secretion.

35. Draw a kidney tubule and a peritubular capillary. Use an arrow to show the direction of movement of substances in tubular secretion.

36. List some important substances that are secreted by the renal tubules.

Metabolism by the Tubules

37. A substance metabolized (synthesized) by the renal tubules that is important in acid-base regulation of urine is _____.

The Concept of Renal Clearance

38. Define renal clearance.

39. The formula for renal clearance is (define each symbol in this formula):

40. The three factors one needs to know before determining clearance of any substance are:

    a.

    b.

    c.

41. Normal clearance values for the following substances are:

    Glucose: $C_G =$ _____

    Inulin: $C_{In} =$ _____

42. The C_{In} is a good indicator of the GFR. Why?

43. What substance that *normally occurs in plasma* is used to approximate the GFR?

    _____

44. If the clearance of a substance is greater than the C_{In}, that substance is filtered and

    _____.

45. If the clearance of a substance is less than the C_{In}, that substance is filtered and

    _____.

MICTURITION

46. The walls of the bladder are made of (*skeletal, smooth*) muscle known as the _____ muscle.

47. The internal urethral sphincter is located _____ and is under (*autonomic, voluntary*) control.

48. The external urethral sphincter is composed of (*skeletal, smooth*) muscle and is under (*autonomic, voluntary*) control.

49. A micturition reflex is elicited when the volume in the urinary bladder reaches approximately _____ ml of urine.

50. Describe the micturition reflex. Be sure to include the receptors, afferent input, spinal cord, efferent output, and effectors.

Review the SECTION SUMMARY and REVIEW QUESTIONS for this section in your textbook.

Section B. Regulation of Sodium, Water, and Potassium Balance

TOTAL-BODY BALANCE OF SODIUM AND WATER

51. The two sources of body water are _____ and _____.

52. Water is lost to the environment via _____, _____, _____ , and _____.

53. Insensible water loss comes from _____ and _____.

54. Sodium and chloride are lost via _____ and _____.

BASIC RENAL PROCESSES FOR SODIUM AND WATER

55. Most of the sodium and water reabsorption occurs in the _____ tubules of the nephron, while most of the *hormonal* regulation occurs in the _____.

56. Sodium reabsorption occurs by _____ transport, while water reabsorption occurs by _____.

Primary Active Sodium Reabsorption

Review Figs. 16–12 and 16–13, page 531.

Coupling of Water Reabsorption to Sodium Reabsorption

57. When sodium is reabsorbed from the renal tubular lumen into the interstitial fluid, the osmolarity of the lumen cells (*increases, decreases*) and the water concentration of the luminal fluid (*increases, decreases*). Simultaneously the osmolarity in the interstitial fluid (*increases, decreases*) and the water concentration (*increases, decreases*). Thus, water moves (*up, down*) its concentration gradient, moving from the _____ into the _____, illustrating the coupling of water reabsorption to sodium reabsorption.

58. The water permeability of the proximal tubule is very (*high, low*).

59. The water permeability of the collecting duct is variable, depending on the peptide hormone _____ released from the _____.

60. Indicate whether an increase (I) or decrease (D) in ADH output would cause the following situations:

    a. _____ urine osmolarity = 70 m*Osm* (hyposmotic), urine output large

    b. _____ urine osmolarity = 700 m*Osm* (hyperosmotic), urine output small

61. A water diuresis is caused by (*low, high*) ADH output.

62. An increase in ADH output (*increases, decreases*) water permeability in the collecting ducts.

63. Describe the disorder diabetes insipidus.

64. How does the cause of the diuresis accompanying diabetes insipidus differ from the cause of the diuresis accompanying diabetes mellitus?

Urine Concentration: The Countercurrent Multiplier System

65. The osmolarity of the tubular fluid *entering* the descending limb of the loop of Henle is _____ mOsmol/L.

66. The osmolarity of the tubular fluid *leaving* the ascending limb of the loop of Henle passing into the collecting duct is about _____ mOsmol/L.

67. The descending limb of the loop of Henle (*does, does not*) actively transport sodium chloride and is very (*permeable, impermeable*) to water, while the ascending limb of the loop of Henle (*does, does not*) actively transport sodium chloride into the interstitial fluid and is very (*permeable, impermeable*) to water.

68. The osmolarities of the descending limb and the interstitial fluid are both (*higher, lower*) than the osmolarity of the ascending limb.

69. The most important component in the loop countercurrent multiplication system is the _____ of sodium chloride in the _____.

70. Renal tubular fluid entering the proximal tubule of the nephron is (*isotonic, hypotonic, hypertonic*) to plasma.

71. Renal tubular fluid in the loop of Henle of the nephron is (*isotonic, hypotonic, hypertonic*) to plasma.

72. Renal tubular fluid in the cortical collecting duct of the nephron is (*isotonic, hypotonic, hypertonic*) to plasma.

73. Why is this countercurrent multiplication system important?

74. Draw a descending and ascending loop of Henle, distal tubule, and collecting duct. Indicate the osmolarities in each of these segments during the production of hyper-osmotic urine.

RENAL SODIUM REGULATION

75. Sodium is filtered by the nephrons and reabsorbed but not _____.

76. Sodium excreted equals sodium filtered minus sodium _____.

77. An increase in dietary sodium will result in a(n) (*increase, decrease*) in sodium filtered, a(n) (*increase, decrease*) in sodium reabsorbed and a(n) (*increase, decrease*) in sodium excreted.

78. Indicate in the following blanks if these parameters would increase (I), decrease (D), or not change (NC) in the presence of high total-body sodium.

    a. _____ plasma volume   c. _____ GFR

    b. _____ blood pressure   d. _____ sodium reabsorption

Control of GFR

79. A decrease in MAP will result in a reflexive (*increase, decrease*) in GFR.

80. A decrease in total-body sodium will result in a reflexive (*increase, decrease*) in GFR.

Control of Sodium Reabsorption

Aldosterone and the renin-angiotensin system

81. By the time the filtrate reaches the collecting ducts, _____ percent of the sodium has been reabsorbed.

82. The steroid hormone aldosterone is an important regulator of sodium reabsorption. This hormone is released from the _____ upon stimulation by _____.

83. Diagram the renin-angiotensin-aldosterone (RAA) system below. Be sure to include renin, angiotensinogen, angiotensin I and II, angiotensin-converting enzyme (ACE), aldosterone, and the organs from which these compounds come. Also indicate if these compounds are peptides or steroids.

84. Describe how the three inputs operate for controlling renin release.

    a. Renal sympathetic nerves:

    b. Intrarenal baroreceptors:

    c. Macula densa:

85. Partial occlusion of a renal artery may lead to (*hypotension, hypertension*). Why?

86. One class of antihypertensive drugs used in treating hypertension are angiotensin-converting enzyme inhibitors (ACE inhibitors). Explain why these drugs are helpful in treating hypertension.

Atrial natriuretic factor

87. ANF is a (*peptide, steroid*) hormone released from _____ and acts on the kidneys to (*increase, decrease*) sodium reabsorption.

RENAL WATER REGULATION

88. Water excretion equals the volume of water _____ minus the volume of water _____ .

89. ADH is a (*peptide, steroid*) hormone produced in the _____ and released from the _____ .

Baroreceptor Control of ADH Secretion

90. Increased baroreceptor afferent firing causes a(n) (*increase, decrease*) in ADH output, and vice versa.

Osmoreceptor Control of ADH Secretion

91. Osmoreceptors, which sense plasma osmolarity, are located in the _____ .

92. An increase in plasma osmolarity causes a(n) (*increase, decrease*) in ADH output to (*increase, decrease*) water permeability in the collecting ducts and (*increases, decreases*) urine volume and (*increases, decreases*) urine osmolarity.

93. Diagram the osmoreceptor control of ADH output in response to severe water deprivation. Include plasma osmolarity, osmoreceptors, ADH, nephron site of action, urine volume, and concentration.

94. Alcohol (*increases, inhibits*) ADH output.

THIRST AND SALT APPETITE

95. Thirst is stimulated by a(n) (*increased, decreased*) extracellular volume and a(n) (*increased, decreased*) plasma osmolarity.

POTASSIUM REGULATION

96. Potassium is the most abundant (*intracellular, extracellular*) ion.

97. Potassium concentrations are important in regulating resting membrane potentials. An increase in extracellular potassium (*depolarizes, hyperpolarizes*) membranes, while a decrease in extracellular potassium _____ membranes.

Renal Regulation of Potassium

98. Potassium is filtered and reabsorbed by the proximal tubule and loop of Henle and _____ by the cortical collecting ducts.

99. An increase in plasma aldosterone directly stimulates the adrenal cortex to increase the output of the steroid hormone _____ , which increases potassium secretion and excretion.

Review Fig. 16-27, page 544.

Review the SECTION SUMMARY and REVIEW QUESTIONS at the end of this section in your textbook.

Section C. Calcium Regulation

100. Changes in plasma calcium change membrane excitability. A decrease in plasma calcium (*increases, decreases*) excitability of nerve- and muscle-cell membranes.

EFFECTOR SITES OF CALCIUM HOMEOSTASIS

101. The regulation of plasma calcium occurs at three major sites in the body:

    a.

    b.

    c.

102. List the three types of bone cells involved in calcium regulation and describe the major function of each:

    a.

    b.

    c.

103. Name a hormone and a vitamin that are involved in plasma calcium regulation.

Kidneys

104. Plasma calcium is _____ and _____ by the kidneys. An increase in plasma calcium reflexively (*increases, decreases*) tubular calcium reabsorption.

GI Tract

105. Calcium is absorbed from the GI tract by _____ transport.

HORMONAL CONTROL

PTH

106. Parathyroid hormone (PTH) is released from the _____ glands, which are located _____, in response to _____.

107. An increase in plasma calcium concentration above the normal level of 10 mg% will lead to a(n) (*increase, decrease*) in PTH output.

108. A decrease in plasma calcium concentration below the normal level of 10 mg% will lead to a(n) (*increase, decrease*) in PTH output.

109. Diagram the negative-feedback loop for the control of plasma calcium levels at about the normal level of 10 mg%. Include the kidneys, GI tract, bone, PTH, and vitamin D.

Vitamin D

110. Name two sources of vitamin D. _____

111. What is the name of the active form of vitamin D? _____

112. Diagram the role of vitamin D in calcium homeostasis.

METABOLIC BONE DISEASES

113. Define osteoporosis.

Review the SECTION SUMMARY and REVIEW QUESTIONS at the end of this section in your textbook.

Section D. Hydrogen-Ion Regulation

114. An increase in arterial hydrogen-ion concentration leads to an (*acidosis, alkalosis*).

115. A decrease in arterial hydrogen-ion concentration leads to an (*acidosis, alkalosis*).

SOURCES OF HYDROGEN-ION GAIN OR LOSS

116. List the major sources by which hydrogen ions can be gained or lost in the body.

    a.

    b.

    c.

    d.

BUFFERING OF HYDROGEN ION IN THE BODY

117. List some major acid-base buffers in the plasma.

    a.

    b.

    c.

    d.

INTEGRATION OF HOMEOSTATIC CONTROLS

118. The primary organs that regulate hydrogen-ion balance are the (*kidneys, lungs*).

119. The respiratory system is a (*rapid, slow*) regulator of hydrogen-ion balance.

RENAL MECHANISMS

120. Renal compensation for hydrogen-ion imbalance is through bicarbonate excretion during (*acidosis, alkalosis*) and through bicarbonate production during (*acidosis, alkalosis*).

Bicarbonate Excretion

121. In the nephrons, bicarbonate is _____ , _____ to a small extent, and excreted.

122. Bicarbonate reabsorption is dependent on _____ secretion.

Review Fig. 16-31, page 544.

Addition of New Bicarbonate to the Plasma

123. Ways of adding new bicarbonate to the plasma include:

    a.

    b.

CLASSIFICATION OF ACIDOSIS AND ALKALOSIS

124. Define:

    a. Respiratory acidosis:

b. Respiratory alkalosis:

c. Metabolic acidosis:

d. Metabolic alkalosis:

125. For the following acid-base disorders, indicate whether there will be an increase (I) or decrease (D) in plasma CO_2, bicarbonate, and hydrogen-ion concentration.

	CO_2	HCO_3	H^+
Respiratory acidosis	a. _____	b. _____	c. _____
Respiratory alkalosis	d. _____	e. _____	f. _____
Metabolic acidosis	g. _____	h. _____	i. _____
Metabolic alkalosis	j. _____	k. _____	l. _____

Review Table 16-8, page 556.

126. How does an increase in $P_{a_{CO_2}}$ lead to an increase in H^+ concentration in arterial blood?

Review the SECTION SUMMARY and REVIEW QUESTIONS at the end of this section in your textbook.

Section E. Diuretics and Kidney Disease

DIURETICS

127. Define diuretics and explain how they work.

128. List two cardiovascular disorders for which diuretics may be used as a prescribed treatment. Explain how these are effective treatments.

a.

b.

129. What is one of the major unwanted side-effects of diuretics?

KIDNEY DISEASE

130. Define uremia.

131. Differentiate between hemodialysis and peritoneal dialysis.

Review the SUMMARY and REVIEW QUESTIONS at the end of this section and the THOUGHT QUESTIONS at the end of this chapter in your textbook.

CHAPTER 16 ANSWER KEY

1. a. regulation of water and inorganic ion balance
    b. removal of metabolic waste products from blood and their excretion in the urine
    c. removal of foreign chemicals from blood and their excretion in the urine
    d. secretion of hormones (erythropoietin, renin, vitamin D_3)
    e. gluconeogenesis

2. See Fig. 16-4, page 521.

3. See Fig. 16-3, page 520.

4. See Fig. 16-1, page 518.

5. Tubular structures of cortical nephrons extend only to the base of the renal pyramid of the medulla. Juxtamedullary nephrons have loops that extend deep into the renal pyramids. Cortical nephrons are approximately seven times more numerous than juxtamedullary nephrons.

6. macula densa, juxtaglomerular cells

7. See Fig. 16.5, page 521.

8. a. glomerular filtration   b. tubular reabsorption   c. tubular secretion

9. protein

10. a. capillary endothelium
    b. basement membrane
    c. epithelial cells (podocytes) of Bowman's capsule

11. Tubular reabsorption is the movement of substances from the tubular lumen to the peritubular capillary. Tubular secretion is movement in the opposite direction—from capillary into the tubular lumen.

12. secreted, reabsorbed

13. 20

14. Glomerular filtrate contains all the substances present in plasma minus the proteins and blood cells.

15. a. glomerular capillary pressure
    b. fluid pressure in Bowman's space
    c. osmotic pressure in glomerular capillary

16. 60

17. 18

18. approx. 150, 125, 180

19. 20 to 25

20. GFR = 180 L/day, and plasma volume = 3 L. Therefore, 3 L × x times/day = 180 L/day and x = 60 times/day.

21. Only the plasma is filtered; formed elements in the blood are not filtered.

22. Filtered load equals GFR × plasma concentration of the substance.

23. 180 L/day × 0.76 g/L = 136.8 g/day

24. The substance is reabsorbed because that which is filtered is greater than that which is excreted; therefore reabsorption has occurred.

25. Reabsorption is the movement of substances from the tubular lumen into the peritubular capillaries.

26. See Fig. 16-6 (#3), page 522.

27. glucose

28. are not

29. diffusion, mediated transport systems

30. diffusion, bulk flow

31. T_m is the maximum transport per unit time for specific substances in the renal tubule. T_m for glucose = 375 mg/min.

32. Filtered load for glucose = 375 mg/100 ml × 180 L/day. Filtered load for glucose = 3.75 g/L × 180 L/day. Filtered load for glucose = 675 g/day or 0.469 g/min or 469 mg/min which exceeds the T_m or transport maximum for glucose of 375 mg/min. Therefore the reabsorption capacity of glucose is exceeded, and glucose appears in the urine.

33. urea. As water is reabsorbed in the proximal tubule, the urea concentration in the proximal tubule increases. Thus, urea passively diffuses down this concentration gradient.

34. Tubular secretion is the movement of substances from the peritubular capillaries into the tubular lumen.

35. See Fig. 6-6 (#2), page 522.

36. hydrogen ions, potassium, choline, creatinine, penicillin

37. ammonium

38. Renal clearance of any substance is the volume of plasma from which that substance is completely cleared by the kidneys per unit time.

39. $C_s = U_s V/P_s$, where C_s = clearance of any substance (s), U_s = urine concentration of s; V = urine volume/time; P_s = plasma concentration of s.

40. a. urine concentration of s
    b. plasma concentration of s
    c. urine volume per unit time

41. 0 ml/min, 125 ml/min

42. Inulin is filtered but not reabsorbed, secreted, or metabolized by the tubule. Therefore, its clearance is equal to the volume of plasma filtered or GFR.

43. creatinine

44. secreted

45. reabsorbed

46. smooth, detrusor

47. at the base or neck of the bladder, autonomic

48. skeletal, voluntary

49. 300 to 400

50. Stretch receptors in the bladder wall, when stimulated, send afferent impulses into the spinal cord which reflexly send parasympathetic efferents firing to the detrusor bladder muscle to cause contraction.

51. metabolically produced water, dietary water

52. skin, respiratory passageways, GI tract, urinary tract

53. skin, respiratory tract lining

54. skin, GI tract

55. proximal, collecting ducts

56. active, diffusion (osmosis)

57. decreases, increases, increases, decreases, down, lumen, interstitial fluid

58. high

59. ADH, posterior pituitary

60. a. D   b. I

61. low

62. increases

63. Diabetes insipidus is a disorder in which there is a decreased output of ADH or an inability to synthesize or release ADH, characterized by a water diuresis (chronic) of up to 25 L/day.

64. The cause of the diuresis in diabetes insipidus is a lack of ADH. The diuresis in diabetes melitus is due to the osmotic pull of water due to the glucose in the urine (or filtrate).

65. 300

66. 100

67. does not, permeable, does, impermeable

68. higher

69. active transport, ascending limb of the loop of Henle

70. isotonic

71. hypertonic

72. hypotonic

73. The countercurrent multiplication system is important because it establishes and maintains the cortical-to-medullary concentration gradient necessary for making a concentrated urine and also generates a "hypotonic" filtrate in the distal convoluted tubule that allows for the generation of dilute urine.

74. See Fig. 16-16, page 535.

75. excreted

76. reabsorbed

77. increase, increase, increase

78. a. I   b. I   c. I   d. D

79. decrease

80. decrease

81. 98

82. adrenal cortex, angiotensin II

83. See Fig. 16-18, page 538.

84. a. Increased sympathetic firing to the juxtaglomerular cells stimulates renin release.
    b. Decreased renal arterial pressure sensed by these intrarenal baroreceptors (juxtaglomerular cells in the walls of the afferent arterioles) stimulates renin release.
    c. Decreased sodium and/or chloride concentration sensed by the macula densa cells (in the JGA where the ascending limb of the loop of Henle comes in contact with the afferent arteriole) stimulates renin release.

85. hypertension. The intrarenal baroreceptors will stimulate increased renin release which will increase aldosterone output, increase sodium reabsorption and plasma volume and blood pressure if the occlusion is of sufficient magnitude.

86. ACE inhibitors block the production of angiotensin II (a powerful vasoconstrictor and stimulator for the release of aldosterone, which in turn causes sodium reabsorption and thus plasma volume, and in turn increases blood pressure). Therefore blocking angiotensin II helps reduce blood pressure.

87. peptide, atria of the heart, decrease

88. filtered, reabsorbed

89. peptide, hypothalamus, posterior pituitary

90. decrease

91. hypothalamus

92. increase, increase, decreases, increases

93. See Fig. 16-22, page 541.

94. inhibits

95. decreased, increased

96. intracellular

97. depolarizes, hyperpolarizes

98. secreted

99. aldosterone

100. increases

101. a. kidneys   b. bone   c. gastrointestinal tract

102. a. osteoglasts—build new bone matrix
    b. osteoclasts—break down bone
    c. osteocytes—are bone cells

103. parathyroid hormone, possibly calcitonin and vitamin D_3

104. filtered, reabsorbed, decreases

105. active

106. parathyroid, on the posterior aspect of the thyroid glands, a decrease in plasma calcium

107. decrease

108. increase

109. See Fig. 16-29, page 549.

110. sun and diet

111. 1,25-dihydroxyvitamin D_3

112. See Fig. 16-30, page 550.

113. Osteoporosis is a condition reflecting abnormal bone metabolism in which there is a degeneration of the bone matrix and a loss of bone minerals.

114. acidosis

115. alkalosis

116. a. metabolic carbon dioxide
    b. organic and inorganic acids from sources other than oxygen
    c. gastrointestinal secretions
    d. kidneys (reabsorption or secretion of hydrogen ions)

117. a. bicarbonate ions   b. phosphate ions   c. proteins   d. hemoglobin

118. kidneys

119. rapid

120. alkalosis, acidosis

121. reabsorbed, secreted

122. hydrogen ion

123. a. hydrogen-ion secretion and excretion of nonbicarbonate buffers such as phosphates
    b. glutamine metabolism with NH_4^+ secretion

124. a. an acidosis due to a respiratory disorder in which there is an accumulation of CO_2
    b. an alkalosis due to a respiratory disorder in which CO_2 is blown off faster than it is produced
    c. an acidosis due to a nonrespiratory cause such as increased lactic acid due to exercise or hypoxia, diarrhea, etc.
    d. an alkalosis due to a nonrespiratory cause such as persistent vomiting with its associated loss of hydrogen ions as HCl from the stomach

125. a. I   d. D   g. D   j. I
    b. I   e. D   h. D   k. I
    c. I   f. D   i. I   l. D

126. Increased $CO_2 + H_2O$ leads to H_2CO_3, which leads to increased H^+ + increased HCO_3^-.

127. Diuretics are drugs used clinically to increase urinary output. They act by inhibiting sodium reabsorption, along with chloride or bicarbonate, resulting in increased excretion of these ions as well as water. Others inhibit hydrogen-ion secretion, block aldosterone action, or block sodium channels.

128. a. congestive heart failure—the increased extracellular volume needs to be eliminated
    b. hypertension—decreases the extracellular volume and "somehow" induces arterial dilation to reduce blood pressure

129. Most of them also increase potassium excretion. Thus potassium supplements are often taken by individuals using diuretics. Low serum potassium may be life-threatening.

130. an accumulation of substances (usually present in the urine) in the blood accompanying severe kidney disorders or diseases; may result in severe toxicity

131. In hemodialysis, the patient's arterial blood is pumped through the dialyzing machine for exchange and "cleansing" and returned to the patient's vein. In peritoneal dialysis, fluid is injected into the patient's abdominal cavity and remains there for several hours, during which time exchange occurs. This dialysis fluid is then removed and replaced with new fluid.

CHAPTER
17
DIGESTION AND ABSORPTION OF FOOD

1. The major structures of the gastrointestinal tract, in order, are:

2. Accessory organs of the gastrointestinal tract include:

3. The four processes associated with gastrointestinal function are:
   a.
   b.
   c.
   d.

OVERVIEW: FUNCTIONS OF THE GASTROINTESTINAL ORGANS

4. Describe briefly the major function of the following:

   a. Mouth:

   b. Salivary glands:

    c. Saliva:

    d. Pharynx:

    e. Esophagus:

    f. Stomach:

    g. Chyme:

    h. Small intestine:

    i. Pancreas:

    j. Liver:

    k. Gallbladder:

    l. Large intestine:

5. The three segments of the small intestine, in order, are:
    a.
    b.
    c.

6. The longest of the three segments is the _____ .

7. Absorption of most of the end products of digestion occurs in the (*first, second, third, fourth*) quarter of the small intestine.

8. The internal diameter and length of the small intestine are about _____ .

9. The internal diameter and length of the large intestine are about _____ .

10. Draw a diagram of the gastrointestinal tract from the mouth through the rectum. Include the accessory glands. Label.

11. The amount of fluid ingested into the gastrointestinal tract per day is about _____ ml.

12. The amount of fluid secreted into the gastrointestinal tract per day is about _____ ml.

13. The amount of fluid lost in the feces per day is about _____ ml.

14. What happens to the majority of fluid entering the gastrointestinal tract by ingestion or secretion each day?

STRUCTURE OF THE GASTROINTESTINAL TRACT WALL

15. The four major layers of the gastrointestinal tract wall from inside to out are:

    a.

    b.

    c.

    d.

16. The layer that contains the circular and longitudinal muscles is the _____ .

17. The fingerlike projections extending inward from the inner surface of the small intestine that increase the surface area for absorption are called _____ , and the single layers of epithelial cells that cover each of these fingerlike projections are called _____ .

18. Draw an intestinal villus. Include and label microvilli, lacteal, and capillary network.

19. Food substances absorbed via the lacteal include _____.

20. Food substances absorbed via the capillary network include _____ .

DIGESTION AND ABSORPTION

Carbohydrate

21. The types of carbohydrates ingested each day include:

22. Starch digestion occurs in the mouth by the enzyme _____ secreted by the _____ glands, and in the small intestine by the pancreatic enzyme _____ and by the intestinal enzyme _____ located in the brush-border membranes of the small intestinal epithelial cells.

23. The end products of starch digestion are _____, which include _____ .

24. Fructose is absorbed across the epithelium by the transport process known as _____ .

25. Glucose and galactose are absorbed across the epithelium by the transport process known as _____ .

Protein

26. The major enzymes that break down proteins into peptides and the source of these enzymes are:

27. Amino acids are transported across the intestinal wall by the transport process known as _____ .

28. Small, intact proteins are able to cross the intestinal epithelium by the processes known as _____ and _____ .

Fat

29. The major enzymes that break down fats into fatty acids and glycerol and the source of these enzymes are:

30. The majority of fat digestion occurs in the _____ .

31. Describe:

    a. Triglyceride:

    b. Diglyceride:

    c. Monoglyceride:

    d. Glycerol:

    e. Phospholipid:

    f. Bile:

    g. Micelle:

    h. Chylomicron:

32. Why and how do fat droplets undergo emulsion?

33. Describe how fats are absorbed from the intestinal lumen into the lacteals of the villi.

Vitamins

34. The fat-soluble vitamins are _____ . They are absorbed in a manner similar to (*carbohydrates, fats, proteins*).

35. The water-soluble vitamins are _____ . They are absorbed by the transport processes of _____ or _____ .

36. Vitamin B_{12} must bind to the protein secreted from the stomach known as _____ for absorption of this vitamin to occur.

37. Absence of vitamin B_{12} results in the condition known as _____ .

Water and Minerals

38. Water absorption in the small intestine occurs primarily by the process known as _____ .

39. Minerals absorbed from the small intestine include:

REGULATION OF GASTROINTESTINAL PROCESSES

40. Regulation of gastrointestinal processes are governed primarily by the _____ and _____ of luminal contents.

Basic Principles

41. Luminal stimuli that initiate gastrointestinal reflexes include:

    a.

    b.

    c.

    d.

Neural regulation

42. Describe the enteric nervous system.

43. Differentiate between short reflexes and long reflexes in the gastrointestinal tract.

Hormonal regulation

44. List four major gastrointestinal hormones. Include the structure and source of each.

Hormone	Structure	Source

   a.

   b.

   c.

   d.

45. Explain the mechanism, providing stimulus, and target organ for each of the above hormones.

   a.

   b.

   c.

   d.

Phases of gastrointestinal control

46. The three phases of gastrointestinal control are:
   a.
   b.
   c.

47. The stimuli that initiate each of these phases are:

    a.

    b.

    c.

Mouth, Pharynx, and Esophagus

Chewing

48. The purpose of chewing is:

Saliva

49. The purpose of salivary secretion into the oral cavity is:

50. Sympathetic and parasympathetic stimulation (*increase, decrease*) salivary secretion.

Swallowing

51. Describe the swallowing reflex. Include the afferent input, the medullary swallowing center, and the efferent output (both somatic and autonomic).

52. Describe peristaltic waves.

53. Draw a diagram indicating where the upper and lower esophageal sphincters are located. These sphincters are composed of _____ muscle.

54. What is heartburn? What are some causes?

Stomach

55. The three major exocrine secretions of the stomach and the cells that secrete each are:

a.

b.

c.

56. The cells that release these secretions are found in the _____ and the _____ of the stomach.

57. The part of the stomach that secretes the hormone gastrin is the _____ .

HCl secretion

58. The primary stimuli for acid secretion into the stomach are:

59. Why does the stomach have a very high acid concentration (low pH) in comparison to the other parts of the gastrointestinal tract?

60. The presence of peptides in the stomach causes the hormone _____ from the _____ to be released into the general circulation, which then stimulates the _____ cells in the _____ of the stomach to (*increase, decrease*) gastric acid secretion.

61. List the factors that affect the intestinal phase or regulation of gastric acid secretion.

Pepsin secretion

62. The inactive precursor of pepsin is _____. The stimulus for activation of this precursor is _____ .

63. The factors that regulate pepsin secretion are _____ .

64. The only substance secreted by the stomach that is absolutely necessary is _____ , secreted by the _____ . This substance is necessary for _____ .

Gastric motility

65. Define receptive relaxation of the stomach.

66. Describe how peristaltic waves cause the stomach to empty its content into the small intestine.

67. Describe the slow waves (basic electrical rhythm) in the longitudinal smooth-muscle layer which establish the frequency of contraction of intestinal smooth muscle.

68. Draw a tracing representing "slow-wave" electrical activity from the small intestine. Add action potentials to these slow waves. Label the X and Y axes and the slow waves and action potentials.

69. What are the differences between the slow waves and the action potentials with respect to function?

70. An increase in stomach volume results in a(n) (*increase, decrease*) in stomach emptying and a(n) (*increase, decrease*) in the force of gastric contractions.

71. An increase in duodenal volume or the presence of fat or hypertonic solutions in the duodenum (*increases, decreases*) gastric emptying.

72. Increased parasympathetic firing (*increases, decreases*) gastrointestinal motility.

73. Increased sympathetic firing (*increases, decreases*) gastrointestinal motility.

Pancreatic Secretions

74. List the major digestive enzymes released from the pancreas and the substrates these enzymes act upon.

    a.

    b.

    c.

    d.

    e.

    f.

    g.

75. Secretin, released from the _____, is the primary stimulus for the release of _____ from the pancreas in response to _____ in the duodenum.

76. CCK, released from the _____, is the primary stimulus for the release of _____ from the pancreas in response to _____ in the duodenum.

77. Diagram feedback loops showing the:
    a. secretin regulation of pancreatic bicarbonate secretion

    b. CCK regulation of pancreatic enzyme secretion

Bile Secretion

78. Diagram the anatomical relationship of the gall bladder, pancreas, and duodenum. Include the pancreatic, hepatic, and common bile ducts and the sphincter of Oddi.

79. List the major components of bile.

80. Describe how bile is involved in fat digestion and absorption.

81. The major bile pigment is _____ and comes from _____.

82. The intestinal hormone that causes bile to be released from the gallbladder is _____. This hormone (*stimulates, inhibits*) contraction of the gallbladder and (*stimulates, inhibits*) the sphincter of Oddi. The stimulus for the release of this hormone is _____.

Small Intestine

Motility

83. Describe the motion or waves that occur in the small intestine *during the digestion of a meal*.

84. What factors influence the *intensity* of segmentation waves?

85. After most of a meal is absorbed, the segmentation waves are replaced by peristaltic wave activity known as _____ . The function of these "intermeal" waves is _____. The hormone that may be responsible for initiating these waves is _____.

86. Define:
Law of the intestine:

Gastroileal reflex:

Intestinointestinal reflex:

Large Intestine

87. Draw the large intestine. Include the ileocecal sphincter; cecum; appendix; ascending, transverse, descending, and sigmoid colon; and rectum.

88. The major colonic secretion is _____.

89. The major function of the large intestine is _____.

90. Substances absorbed from the colon include _____ .

91. Gas (flatus) in the colon comes from _____ .

Motility and defecation

92. The segmentation rate (rhythm) in the colon is (*faster than, equal to, slower than*) that in the small intestine.

93. Material can normally remain in the colon for _____ h.

94. Describe:

    Mass movement:

    Defecation reflex:

95. The contents of fecal material include:

PATHOPHYSIOLOGY OF THE GASTROINTESTINAL TRACT

Ulcers

96. Various types of gastrointestinal ulcers include _____ .
    The most common type of ulcer is _____ .

97. Some factors that may cause ulcers include:

Vomiting

98. Why is excessive vomiting dangerous?

Gallstones

99. How are gallstones formed?

100. What are some of the major physiological effects that occur when a gallstone blocks the common bile duct?

Lactose Intolerance

101. Describe the effects associated with lactose intolerance.

Constipation and Diarrhea

102. Some of the mechanisms by which laxatives increase the frequency or ease of defecation are:

103. The serious or even life-threatening consequences of prolonged diarrhea are:

Review the SUMMARY, REVIEW QUESTIONS, and THOUGHT QUESTIONS at the end of this chapter in your textbook.

CHAPTER 17 ANSWER KEY

1. mouth, pharynx, esophagus, stomach, small intestine, large intestine

2. salivary glands, liver, gallbladder, pancreas

3. a. digestion   b. secretion   c. absorption   d. motility

4. a. chews food, breaks food into smaller pieces, site of initiation of carbohydrate digestion
   b. three pairs of exocrine glands that release saliva into the oral cavity to initiate carbohydrate digestion and to moisten food
   c. secretion from salivary glands containing mucus to moisten food and amylase, an enzyme, which acts on polysaccharides in beginning carbohydrate digestion
   d. conducting pathway from mouth to esophagus
   e. conducting pathway for food from pharynx to stomach
   f. temporary storage area for food, site of protein digestion due to the secretion from the stomach wall of the enzyme pepsin and hydrochloric acid
   g. the solution (toothpaste consistency) of foodstuffs leaving the stomach consisting of small proteins, polysaccharides, and fat droplets
   h. site of final stages of digestion and most absorption of end products of food digestion (amino acids, fatty acids, and monosaccharides)
   i. exocrine organ that secretes digestive enzymes and bicarbonate ions into the small intestine
   j. secretes bile that contains bile salts which help solubilize dietary fat
   k. a small sac under the liver that stores and concentrates bile from the liver and releases it into the small intestine when the gallbladder contracts
   l. temporary storage site of undigested or unabsorbed material, site of compaction of this material

5. a. duodenum   b. jejunum   c. ileum

6. ileum

7. first

8. $1\frac{1}{2}$ in $\times$ 9 ft

9. $2\frac{1}{2}$ in $\times$ 4 ft

10. See Fig. 17-1, page 562.

11. 1200

12. 7000

13. 100

14. It is absorbed into the blood.

15. a. mucosa   b. submucosa   c. muscularis externa   d. serosa

16. muscularis externa

17. villi, microvilli

18. See Fig. 17-7, page 569.

19. fats

20. monosaccharides and amino acids

21. Starches (two-thirds), sucrose (table sugar), lactose (milk sugar), monosaccharides, cellulose

22. amylase, salivary, amylase, amylase

23. monosaccharides; glucose, galactose, fructose

24. facilitated diffusion

25. secondary active transport coupled to sodium

26. pepsin (stomach), trypsin and chymotrypsin (pancreas), carboxypeptidase (pancreas), aminopeptidase (small intestine)

27. secondary active transport

28. endocytosis, exocytosis

29. lipase (pancreas), lipase (small intestine)

30. small intestine

31. a. glycerol molecule with three fatty acid chains attached
    b. glycerol molecule with two fatty acid chains attached
    c. glycerol molecule with one fatty acid chain attached
    d. three-carbon molecule (alcohol)
    e. lipid that contains a phosphate group
    f. fluid from the liver that is stored and concentrated by the gallbladder and is essential for fat absorption
    g. very small water-soluble particle composed of fatty acids, phospholipids, and glycerides, which can be absorbed into the villi
    h. tiny, protein-coated droplet containing triglycerides, cholesterol, and free fatty acids

32. Fat droplets are emulsified by bile salts into smaller droplets, increasing the surface area for lipase activity.

33. Fats enter the small intestine and are emulsified by bile salts. Pancreatic and intestinal lipases break the fats down into fatty acids. These fatty acids combine with bile salts,

phospholipids, and glycerides to form micelles. Micelles are absorbed into the villi epithelial cells where the fatty acids are resynthesized in the endoplasmic reticulum into triglycerides. These fats assume a protein coat and become chylomicrons and are released into the central lacteal of each villus.

34. A, D, E, and K; fats

35. B complex and C, diffusion, carrier-mediated transport

36. intrinsic factor

37. pernicious anemia

38. osmosis

39. sodium, chloride, bicarbonate, potassium, magnesium, calcium, ion, zinc, iodide

40. volume, composition

41. a. lumen wall distention
    b. chyme osmolarity
    c. chyme acidity
    d. chyme concentrations of monosaccharides, fatty acids, peptides, and amino acids

42. The enteric nervous system is located as a plexus between the longitudinal and circular muscles of the digestive tract and helps regulate the rhythmic contraction of the smooth muscles. It receives both sympathetic and parasympathetic input.

43. Short reflexes are reflex arcs that have their receptors in the wall and that send information through the nerve plexus to the effector cells in the wall. Long reflexes have their receptors in the GI wall as well, but send their information to the CNS by afferent fibers and back to the nerve plexus by autonomic nerve fibers.

44. a. gastrin   peptide   stomach (antrum)
    b. secretin   peptide   small intestine
    c. CCK   peptide   small intestine
    d. GIP   peptide   small intestine

45. a. Gastrin: increases gastric secretions; stimulus for gastrin release is presence of food in antrum of stomach, especially peptides.
    b. Secretin: increases watery HCO_3^--rich secretion from pancreas; stimulus for secretin release from duodenum is acid in small intestine.
    c. CCK: increases pancreatic enzyme secretion; stimulus for CCK release is amino acids and fatty acids in small intestine.
    d. GIP: stimulates insulin secretion from the pancreas; stimulus for GIP release is glucose or fat in the small intestine.
    See Table 17-3, page 577.

46. a. cephalic   b. gastric   c. intestinal

47. a. cephalic: sight, smell, taste, or chewing of food
    b. gastric: stomach distention, low acidity, peptides
    c. intestinal: distention, high acidity, osmolarity, end products of digestion

48. to break up foodstuffs into small particles for swallowing, moisten and lubricate food for swallowing, mix saliva with food to initiate carbohydrate digestion

49. to moisten and lubricate food, initiate carbohydrate digestion

50. increase

51. The food passes from the oral cavity into the pharynx. Afferent impulses are sent to the swallowing center in the medulla via the glossopharyngeal (IX) nerve. Output from the medulla sends a regulated sequence of impulses to the muscles of the pharynx, esophagus, stomach, and breathing muscles.

52. waves of contraction in the muscle layer of the gastrointestinal tract that aid in moving food from the oral to the anal end of the food tract

53. skeletal. See Fig. 17-15, page 580.

54. Heartburn is the reflex of acidic gastric contents from the stomach into the esophagus causing pain as if over the heart. Some causes are a weakened lower esophageal sphincter, forceful abdominal compression after eating, and pregnancy.

55. a. hydrochloric acid (parietal cells)
    b. pepsinogen (chief cells)
    c. mucus (tubular mucus cells)

56. body, fundus

57. antrum

58. presence of peptides in the stomach, low H^+ concentration, increased gastrin release, large amounts of calcium in the stomach

59. The stomach needs a very high acid concentration for the acid hydrolysis of proteins into peptides and for the activation of inactive pepsinogen into active pepsin. (Optimum pH for pepsin is approx. 2.)

60. gastrin, antrum, parietal and chief, body and fundus, increase

61. High acid content in the small intestine reflexively inhibits acid secretion.
    Distention of the small intestine increases gastric acid secretions.
    Hypertonic solutions in the small intestine increase acid secretions.
    Solutions containing amino acids, free fatty acids, and monosaccharides inhibit gastric acid secretions.
    Enterogastrone inhibits gastric acid secretions.

62. pepsinogen, an acid environment

63. the same as those that regulate acid secretion

64. intrinsic factor, parietal cells, absorption of vitamin B_{12}

65. Smooth muscles in the fundus and body of the stomach relax before the arrival of food from the mouth and esophagus, thus allowing an increase in stomach volume.

66. A weak peristaltic wave moves the stomach contents toward the antrum of the stomach. When the contents reach the more muscular antrum, more powerful contractions occur that propel the chyme through the pyloric sphincter. A few milliliters of chyme are pumped through the pyloric sphincter with each wave.

67. These slow waves (approx. three per minute) are generated by pacemaker cells that undergo spontaneous depolarization-repolarization cycles (basic electrical rhythm). In the absence of neural or hormonal input, these depolarizations do not reach threshold to fire action potentials required to elicit contractions.

68. See Fig. 17-21, page 585.

69. Slow waves establish the *frequency* of contraction, and the action potentials establish the *force* of contraction.

70. increase, increase

71. decreases

72. increases

73. decreases

74. a. trypsin   (proteins)
    b. chymotrypsin   (proteins)
    c. carboxypeptidases   (proteins)
    d. lipases   (fats)
    e. amylases   (polysaccharides)
    f. ribonucleases   (nucleic acids)
    g. deoxyribonucleases   (nucleic acids)

75. duodenum, bicarbonate, acid

76. duodenum, enzymes, fatty acids, and amino acids

77. a. See Fig. 17-25, page 588.
    b. See Fig. 17-26, page 588.

78. See Fig. 17-4, page 566.

79. bile salts, cholesterol, lecithin, bicarbonate, bile pigments, trace metals

80. Bile emulsifies larger fat globules into small fat globules and bile acids in forming micelles for fatty acid absorption into the villi.

81. bilirubin, heme part of hemoglobin during erythrocyte breakdown

82. CCK, stimulates, inhibits, presence of fat in the duodenum

83. These are segmentation waves that are rhythmic, stationary contractions and relaxations that divide and subdivide intestinal contents.

84. hormones, enteric nervous system, autonomic nervous system. [Parasympathetic increases activity (intensity) and sympathetic decreases intensity.]

85. migrating motor complexes, move along undigested or unabsorbed food into large intestine, motilin

86. Law of the intestine: intestinal distention results in contraction of the smooth muscle on the oral side of the distention and relaxation of smooth muscle at the anal end, resulting in movement of material toward the large intestine.

    Gastroileal reflex: a reflex in which gastric emptying increases segmental intensity in the ileum (a feedforward reflex).

    Intestinointestinal reflex: a reflex in which intestinal distention, injury, or infection can lead to decreased motility in the intestine.

87. See Fig. 17-31, page 592.

88. mucus

89. storage and compaction of fecal material

90. sodium, H_2O (osmosis), vitamins

91. bacterial action on undigested starches that cannot be digested by intestinal enzymes

92. slower than

93. 18 to 24

94. Mass movement: waves of intense spreading over the colon toward the rectum three to four times each day
Defecation reflex: reflex that consists of contraction of rectum, relaxation of the internal and sphincter, increased peristaltic activity in the sigmoid colon, and eventual relaxation of the external and sphincter that allows feces to be expelled

95. water, bacteria, undigested polysaccharides, bile pigments, cholesterol, and electrolytes, especially potassium

96. esophageal, gastric, and duodenal; duodenal

97. genetic susceptibility, drugs, alcohol, bile salts, excessive secretion of acid and pepsin, *Helicobacer pylori* bacterium, gastritis, stress-induced increase in acid secretion

98. There may be a large loss of water and salts that would normally be reabsorbed from the small intestine. This can lead to severe dehydration, altered electrolyte levels, acid-base imbalance, cardiovascular disturbances.

99. Elevated levels of cholesterol (or bile pigments) in the bile may crystallize out.

100. Absence of bile may lead to decreased fat digestion and absorption; fat may appear in the feces, leading to diarrhea; absence of pancreatic secretions results in inability to neutralize the acid load or digest completely the nutrients, which may lead to a nutritional deficiency; buildup of bilirubin in the blood may cause a jaundice appearance.

101. In the absence of lactase, lactose is not broken down into galactose and glucose for absorption by the small intestine. Therefore lactose appears in the large intestine where bacteria acts upon it and large volumes of gas may be produced. There may also be an osmotic diarrhea.

102. Dietary fiber increases water retention in the colon; mineral oil lubricates feces; magnesium and aluminum salts increase water retention in the colon; castor oil stimulates colon motility.

103. decreases blood volume, potassium depletion, metabolic acidosis

CHAPTER
18
REGULATION OF ORGANIC METABOLISM, GROWTH, AND ENERGY BALANCE

Section A. Control and Integration of Carbohydrate, Protein, and Fat Metabolism

EVENTS OF THE ABSORPTIVE AND POSTABSORPTIVE STATES

1. Define:

   a. Absorptive state:

   b. Postabsorptive state:

2. The average time required for complete absorption of a meal is _____ h.

Absorptive State

3. The three major nutrients that are present in foodstuffs are _____, _____, and _____ . The end products of digestion of these nutrients are, respectively, _____ , _____ , and _____ .

4. The substances absorbed from the gastrointestinal tract into the blood that pass directly to the liver via the hepatic portal vein are _____ and _____. The _____ are absorbed into the_____, which then empties into the general circulation.

Absorbed glucose

5. The three major fates of glucose during the absorptive phase are:

   a.

   b.

   c.

6. In the liver, the glucose that is synthesized into triacylglycerols can be packaged with proteins to be secreted into the blood as _____ .

7. The VLDL complex (*does, does not*) readily penetrate capillary walls.

8. The VLDL triacylglycerols in the blood are hydrolyzed into _____ and by the capillary enzyme _____. This enzyme is in high concentrations in _____ tissue. Thus the fatty acids generated in adipose tissue can be re-synthesized into _____ for storage.

Absorbed triacylglycerols

9. Triacylglycerols are absorbed from the gastrointestinal tract into the _____ in the form of _____. The fatty acids are released from the chylomicron triacylglycerols by the enzyme _____.

10. When triacylglycerols are formed, the source of the α-glycerol phosphate is _____ .

11. Three major sources of fatty acids found in adipose tissue triacylglycerols are:

    a.

    b.

    c.

Absorbed amino acids

12. Most of the absorbed amino acids enter _____ cells and are used for _____. Excess amino acids are converted to _____ or _____ .

Review Table 18-1, page 606, and Fig. 18-1, page 603.

Postabsorptive State

Sources of blood glucose

13. Blood glucose is generated during the postabsorptive state by:

    a.

    b.

    c.

14. The end products of glycogenolysis in the liver and skeletal muscle are _____ and _____ , respectively.

15. The breakdown of liver glycogen is an immediate source of blood glucose but can supply only about _____h of caloric energy.

16. Using a diagram, show how muscle glycogen can eventually be a source of blood glucose.

17. Using a diagram, show how triacylglycerols can be a source of blood glucose.

18. Using a diagram, show how proteins can be a source of blood glucose.

19. The synthesis of glucose from nonglucose precursors (*pyruvate, lactate, glycerol, amino acids*) is known as _____. The primary organ where this occurs is the _____.

Glucose sparing (fat utilization)

20. In the transition from the absorptive to the postabsorptive state, glucose use is reduced and _____ utilization is increased. This metabolic adjustment is called _____.

21. Outline the catabolism of triacylglycerols (in adipose tissue).

22. The liver, unlike most other cells in the body, converts acetyl CoA from fatty acid metabolism into _____ which can be used as a source of energy during fasting and glucose sparing.

23. Summarize how plasma glucose can remain nearly normal after several days of fasting.

ENDOCRINE AND NEURAL CONTROL OF THE ABSORPTIVE AND POSTABSORPTIVE STATES

Insulin

24. Insulin is a (*peptide, steroid, amine*) hormone released from the _____ cells of the _____ located in the pancreas. Its major effect is to (*raise, lower*) blood glucose by facilitating the transport of glucose into cells. This is similar to the events that occur during the (*absorptive, postabsorptive*) state.

25. The major target organs (or cells) for insulin are:

Effects on muscle and adipose tissue

26. Glucose enters most cells by the transport process known as _____.

27. Insulin facilitates the uptake of glucose by muscle and fat cells by _____.

28. In muscle cells, insulin (*favors, inhibits*) glycolysis, (*favors, inhibits*) glycogen synthesis, (*stimulates, inhibits*) glycogen synthase, and (*stimulates, inhibits*) glycogen phosphorylase.

29. In fat cells, insulin (*favors, inhibits*) triacylglycerol synthesis, and (*favors, inhibits*) intracellular lipase.

30. Insulin (*favors, inhibits*) cellular uptake of amino acids into most cells.

31. Overall, insulin favors (*anabolic, catabolic*) effects. This resembles the (*absorptive, postabsorptive*) state.

Effects on liver

32. As in muscle and adipose tissue, insulin's effects on the liver favor glycogen (*synthesis, breakdown*) and triacylglycerol (*synthesis, breakdown*).

33. Insulin's specific effects on liver, not seen in muscle and adipose tissue, include:

   a.

   b.

34. Insulin influences glucose uptake in liver cells by:

   a.

   b.

   c.

Effects of decreases in plasma insulin concentration

35. List six major metabolic effects brought about by a decrease in plasma insulin concentration.

    a.

    b.

    c.

    d.

    e.

    f.

36. Metabolic effects seen with a *decrease* in plasma insulin reflect the same metabolic effects that are seen during the (*absorptive, postabsorptive*) state.

37. Metabolic effects seen with an *increase* in plasma insulin reflect the same metabolic effects that are seen during the (*absorptive, postabsorptive*) state.

Control of insulin secretion

38. Diagram the feedback loop for the control of insulin secretion.

39. Explain how glucose-dependent insulinotropic hormone (GIP) controls insulin secretion.

40. Explain how the autonomic nervous system influences insulin secretion.

Glucagon

41. The major stimulus for the release of glucagon is _____.

42. Glucagon (*increases, decreases*) plasma glucose and ketones.

43. Glucagon's effects on the liver include:
    a.
    b.
    c.

44. During the absorptive state the glucagon/insulin ratio is (*high, low*), while during the postabsorptive state this ratio is (*high, low*).

45. Sympathetic and parasympathetic innervation of alpha cells in the islets of Langerhans in the pancreas (*increases, decreases*) glucagon secretion.

Epinephrine and Sympathetic Nerves to Liver and Adipose Tissue

46. Epinephrine and sympathetic innervation to the pancreas (*increases, decreases*) insulin secretion and (*increases, decreases*) glucagon secretion.

47. Epinephrine and sympathetic innervation to the liver and adipose tissue increases (I) or decreases (D) the following:
    a. _____ glycogenolysis in liver and skeletal muscle
    b. _____ gluconeogenesis in liver
    c. _____ lipolysis in adipocytes

Other Hormones

Cortisol

48. Cortisol enhances metabolic effects (*similar to, opposite*) those of insulin.

Growth hormone

49. Growth hormone enhances metabolic effects (*similar to, opposite*) those of insulin.

50. Hormones that increase plasma glucose levels are:

51. Hormones that decrease plasma glucose levels are: _____

52. Hormones that increase during the absorptive state are: _____

53. Hormones that increase during the postabsorptive state are: _____

FUEL HOMEOSTASIS IN EXERCISE AND STRESS

54. What happens to plasma glucose levels during mild exercise?

55. What happens to plasma glucose levels during severe exercise?

56. Graph plasma glucose, glucagon, and insulin concentrations during prolonged moderate exercise (250 min). Plot plasma levels on the Y axis and time on the X axis.

DIABETES MELLITUS

57. Differentiate between insulin-dependent diabetes mellitus (IDDM) and non-insulin-dependent diabetes mellitus (NIDDM).

58. An individual with untreated IDDM has an increase (I) or decrease (D) in the following:
    a. _____ plasma glucose
    b. _____ glycogenolysis (liver)
    c. _____ gluconeogenesis (liver)
    d. _____ lipolysis
    e. _____ plasma glycerol and fatty acids
    f. _____ plasma ketones
    g. _____ urinary glucose
    h. _____ urinary ketones
    i. _____ urine volume
    j. _____ blood pH

59. A major factor that may predispose an individual to NIDDM is:

REGULATION OF PLASMA CHOLESTEROL

60. List some functions of cholesterol in the body.

61. Why are high plasma cholesterol levels dangerous?

62. Two sources of plasma cholesterol are:
    a.
    b.

63. What is the liver's role in cholesterol metabolism?

64. Cholesterol synthesis by the liver is (*increased, decreased*) when dietary cholesterol is increased because cholesterol (*stimulates, inhibits*) the enzyme critical for cholesterol synthesis by the liver.

65. Diagram the feedback loop involved in maintaining normal plasma cholesterol in the face of dietary cholesterol changes.

66. Animal fat is a major source of (*saturated, unsaturated*) fatty acids that (*increase, decrease*) plasma cholesterol levels.

67. Plant oils are a major source of (*saturated, unsaturated*) fatty acids that (*increase, decrease*) plasma cholesterol levels.

68. Plasma cholesterol levels are altered by altering cholesterol

    a.

    b.

    c.

69. A "healthy" plasma cholesterol level is approx. _____ mg/dl.

70. Cholesterol is carried in plasma as:

    a.

    b.

    c.

    d.

71. (*HDLs, LDLs*) carry cholesterol to cells.

72. (*HDLs, LDLs*) remove cholesterol from cells.

73. "Good" cholesterol is carried by (*HDLs, LDLs*), and "bad" cholesterol is carried by (*HDLs, LDLs*).

74. The (*higher, lower*) the LDL/HDL ratio, the lower the risk of developing athero-sclerotic heart disease.

75. Indicate whether the following increase (I) or decrease (D) circulating levels of HDLs:
    a. _____ exercise
    b. _____ cigarette smoking
    c. _____ estrogens

Review the SUMMARY and REVIEW QUESTIONS at the end of this section in your textbook.

Section B. Control of Growth

BONE GROWTH

76. Describe how long bones grow in length.

77. Long bones continue to grow until _____ occurs.

ENVIRONMENTAL FACTORS INFLUENCING GROWTH

78. The major environmental factors that influence growth are:
    a.
    b.

HORMONAL INFLUENCES ON GROWTH

Growth Hormone

79. Describe the major effects of growth hormone on postnatal growth of long bones. Include IGF-1 (somatomedin C).

80. Overproduction of growth hormone during childhood may result in the condition known as _____, while overproduction of growth hormone in adults after epipyseal closure may result in the condition known as _____.

81. Dwarfism may be caused by:
    a.
    b.
    c.

82. Growth hormone stimulates long-bone growth indirectly via the mediator known as _____ but stimulates protein synthesis directly.

Review Table 18-4, page 616.

83. Diagram the feedback loop for the release of growth hormone.

84. Other hormones that increase growth hormone secretion are _____ and _____.

85. Plasma growth hormone is (*higher, lower*) during sleep and (*higher, lower*) during the day.

86. The 24-h secretion rate of growth hormone is highest in (*children, adolescents, adults*).

Thyroid Hormones

87. Infants and children who are hypothyroid are short of stature. Why?

88. Thyroid hormones play an important permissive role in central nervous system development. How would the CNS of a hypothyroid newborn be affected?

Insulin

89. How does insulin help promote growth?

Sex Hormones

90. How do sex hormones help promote growth?

91. How do sex hormones ultimately stop bone growth?

92. How do testosterone-like agents (anabolic steroids) increase muscle mass?

Cortisol

93. The *antigrowth* effects of cortisol are due to:

Review Table 18-5, page 627.

Review the SUMMARY and REVIEW QUESTIONS at the end of this section in your textbook.

Section C. Regulation of Total-Body Energy Balance and Temperature

BASIC CONCEPTS OF ENERGY EXPENDITURE AND CALORIC BALANCE

94. When organic molecules are broken down, the energy liberated can appear either as
_____ or _____.

95. Complete this equation: $\Delta E = $ ___ + ____ .

96. Approximately _____ percent of energy released during metabolism appears as heat.

97. Total energy expenditure = heat + _____ + _____ .

Metabolic Rate

98. Define:

   a. Metabolic rate:

   b. Kilocalorie (kcal):

Determinants of Metabolic Rate

Basal metabolic rate (BMR)

99. Define BMR.

100. A child's BMR is (*equal to, greater than, less than*) an adult's BMR.

101. A female's BMR is (*equal to, greater than, less than*) a male's BMR.

102. A pregnant woman's BMR is (*equal to, greater than, less than*) a nonpregnant woman's BMR.

103. Indicate whether the following will cause an individual's metabolic rate to increase (I) or decrease (D):

   a. _____ thyroid hormones   c. _____ food ingestion

   b. _____ epinephrine   d. _____ skeletal muscle activity

Total-Body Energy Balance

104. Energy from food ingested = _____ + _____ + _____.

Control of Food Intake

105. Diagram the inputs that control food intake. Indicate which inputs stimulate hunger (+) and which inhibit (−) hunger.

Obesity

106. What is your "desirable" body weight?

107. According to the body mass index (BMI), do you fall within the normal range? Include the formula for BMI.

108. Obesity is defined as _____ percent over the desirable body weight.

109. Two valuable components in a sensible weight loss program include:

    a.

    b.

110. If an individual's metabolic rate for 24 h is 2400 kcal and the dietary intake is 1500 kcal/day, how many grams of body fat will be burned per day? Show your work.

111. How long will it take for this individual to lose 1 lb of body weight? Show your work.

Eating Disorders: Anorexia Nervosa and Bulimia

112. Differentiate between anorexia nervosa and bulimia.

REGULATION OF BODY TEMPERATURE

Mechanisms of Heat Loss or Gain

113. State and briefly describe four mechanisms by which the body can lose heat to the external environment.

a.

b.

c.

d.

Temperature-Regulating Reflexes

114. Diagram the temperature-regulating mechanisms involved in regulating body temperature. Start with the peripheral thermoreceptors and central thermoreceptors. Include efferent output and effectors.

Control of heat production

115. The major control of heat production for temperature regulation is _____.
     This results in an increase in internal heat and is thus known as _____.

Control of heat loss by radiation and conduction

116. Ways of regulating heat loss by radiation and conduction are:

Control of heat loss by evaporation

117. Describe insensible water loss.

118. Differentiate between the cooling effect of sweating on a humid day versus a non-humid day.

Integration of effector mechanisms

119. Core body temperature can be regulated in environmental temperatures in the thermoneutral zone by _____.

120. Environmental temperatures above the thermoneutral zone require the body to compensate by _____.

121. Environmental temperatures below the thermoneutral zone require the body to compensate by _____.

Temperature Acclimatization

Acclimatization to heat

122. During heat acclimatization, there is a(n) (*increase, decrease*) in the volume of sweat produced. There is also a decrease in the loss of sodium in sweat due to the increase in the hormone _____ .

Acclimatization to cold

123. One of the major factors in cold acclimatization is _____ .

Fever

124. During fever, the hypothalamic set-point for temperature regulation is reset. The basis for this "resetting" may be:

125. The hyperthermia accompanying exercise is due to _____ .

Review the SUMMARY and REVIEW QUESTIONS at the end of this section and the THOUGHT QUESTIONS at the end of this chapter in your textbook.

CHAPTER 18 ANSWER KEY

1. a. time during which nutrients are entering the blood from the GI tract
   b. time during which the GI tract is empty of nutrients and must be supplied from body stores

2. four

3. carbohydrates, fats, proteins, monosaccharides, fatty acids, amino acids

4. monosaccharides, amino acids, fatty acids, lymph system

5. a. used as a source of energy
   b. stored as glycogen in liver and skeletal muscle
   c. stored as fat in adipose tissue

6. very low-density lipoproteins (VLDL)

7. does not

8. fatty acids, monoglycerides, lipoprotein lipase, adipose, triacylglycerides

9. lymph system, chylomicrons, lipoprotein lipase

10. glucose metabolism

11. a. glucose that enters adipose tissue and is converted to fatty acids
    b. glucose that is converted to VLDL triacylglycerols and then transported to adipose tissue
    c. ingested triacylglycerols that are transported as chylomicrons

12. all body cells (especially muscle cells), protein synthesis, carbohydrates, fats

13. a. glycogenolysis   b. lipolysis   c. gluconeogenesis

14. glucose, glucose 6-phosphate

15. 4

16. See Fig. 18-2, page 604.

17. See Fig. 18-2, page 604.

18. See Fig. 18-2, page 604.

19. gluconeogenesis, liver

20. fat, glucose sparing

21. See Fig. 18-2, page 604.

22. ketones

23. This is due to the combined effects of glycogenolysis, gluconeogenesis, and the switch to fat utilization (or glucose sparing). The glucose is "spared" so the nervous system can use it while most other cells of the body shift to fat metabolism.

24. peptide, beta, islets of Langerhans, lower, absorptive

25. cardiac and skeletal muscle, adipose tissue, and liver

26. facilitated diffusion

27. affecting the glucose transporter proteins

28. inhibits, favors, stimulates, inhibits

29. favors, inhibits

30. favors

31. anabolic, absorptive

32. synthesis, synthesis

33. a. inhibition of gluconeogenesis
    b. not influencing the facilitated diffusion glucose transport mechanism as it does in muscle and adipocytes

34. a. stimulating glucokinase (phosphorylates glucose to glucose 6-phosphate)
    b. inhibiting glucose 6-phosphatase
    c. a and b above keep the cytosol glucose concentration low so glucose will move down its concentration gradient, which is required in facilitated diffusion transport

35. a. net protein catabolism in muscle
    b. net glycogen catabolism in all target cells
    c. net fat catabolism in adipose tissue
    d. decrease in glycolysis and decreased activity of glycolytic enzymes
    e. increased utilization of fatty acids and ketones
    f. gluconeogenesis and release of glucose from the liver

36. postabsorptive

37. absorptive

38. See Fig. 18-6, page 612.

39. GIP is secreted by the GI tract in response to eating, and it stimulates the release of insulin. This is a feedforward component for an "early" rise in insulin secretion.

40. Activity of the parasympathetic nervous system during the ingestion of a meal stimulates insulin secretion. Activity of the sympathetic nervous system (or increased plasma epinephrine) inhibits insulin secretion.

41. decreased plasma glucose

42. increases

43. a. increased glycogen breakdown
    b. increased gluconeogenesis
    c. synthesis of ketones

44. low, high

45. increases

46. decreases, increases

47. a. I   b. I   c. I

48. opposite

49. opposite

50. glucagon, epinephrine, cortisol, growth hormone

51. insulin

52. insulin

53. glucagon and epinephrine

54. There is very little change or a slight increase because the liver acts as a source of glucose.

55. There is a decrease in plasma glucose.

56. See Fig. 18-11, page 617.

57. IDDM (type I): there is a decrease in insulin output from the pancreas, resulting in a decrease in plasma insulin levels. Insulin is essential as a treatment. NIDDM (type II): insulin may be at normal or near-normal physiological levels. Insulin is not required for treatment. Dietary changes may be necessary, and sometimes agents that stimulate lazy beta cells to produce insulin (sulfonylureas) are required. Exercise is also encouraged.

58. a. I   d. I   g. I
    b. I   e. I   h. I
    c. I   f. I   i. D

59. obesity which may lead to target cell insulin resistance or a defect in beta cell function

60. precursor of plasma membrane compounds, bile salts, steroid hormones, and other specialized molecules

61. They may lead to atherosclerotic placques, which can lead to heart attacks, strokes, etc.

62. a. synthesis within the body (endogenous)   b. dietary (exogenous)

63. The liver can synthesize cholesterol or remove cholesterol from the blood and secrete it in bile or metabolize it into bile salts.

64. decreased, inhibits

65. See Fig. 18-13, page 621.

66. saturated, increase

67. unsaturated, decrease

68. a. synthesis   b. excretion   c. metabolism to bile salts

69. 200 or less

70. a. chylomicrons   b. VLDLs   c. LDLs   d. HDLs

71. LDLs

72. HDLs

73. HDLs, LDLs

74. lower

75. a. I   b. D   c. I

76. At the distal ends of bones (epiphyses) there is an epiphyseal growth plate where osteoblasts convert cartilage into bone and new bone is thus laid down.

77. epiphyseal closure

78. a. adequate nutrient supply
    b. adequate health (lack of disease)

79. Growth hormone stimulates chondrocyte differentiation in the epiphyseal plates into mature chondrocytes. During chondrocyte differentiation and maturation, IGF-1 is secreted and cells become responsive to IGF-1. IGF-1 stimulates chondrocytes to undergo mitosis and thus allow for bone formation.

80. giantism, acromegaly

81. a. decreased GH secretion
    b. decreased IGF-1 production
    c. failure of the tissues to respond to IGF-1

82. IGF-1

83. See Fig. 10-23, page 297.

84. thyroid hormones, sex hormones

85. higher, lower

86. adolescents

87. Thyroid hormones are required for the synthesis and growth-promoting effects of GH.

88. There would be decreased CNS development that may lead to mental retardation but may be reversible if treated during the first few months of extrauterine life (with thyroid hormones).

89. Insulin is an anabolic hormone and stimulates amino acid uptake and protein synthesis. It exerts growth-promoting effects on cell differentiation. It increases mitosis during fetal life. It stimulates IGF-1 secretion during childhood.

90. They stimulate GH secretion.

91. They induce epiphyseal closure.

92. They have a direct anabolic effect on protein synthesis.

93. inhibition of DNA synthesis, increased protein catabolism, inhibition of bone growth, stimulation of osteoclast activity and inhibition of osteoblast activity, thus encouraging bone breakdown

94. heat, work

95. *H, W*

96. 60

97. external work, stored energy

98. a. total energy expenditure per unit time
    b. unit of energy: amount of heat required to heat 1 L of water 1°C

99. Basal metabolic rate is the metabolic rate recorded when an individual is at complete mental and physical rest in a comfortable temperature and has been in a fasted state for at least 12 h.

100. greater than

101. less than

102. greater than

103. a. I   b. I   c. I   d. I

104. external work, internal heat production, energy stored

105. See Fig. 18-18, page 635.

106. Use Table 18-11 on page 636 of your textbook.

107. BMI = weight (kg)/height (m²); BMI (normal range) for adults = 19 to 25; BMI > 27.8 for men indicates obesity; BMI> 27.3 for women indicates obesity.

108. 20

109. a. exercise   b. dietary changes

110. There are 3500 kcal/lb of body fat. 2400 kcal − 1500 kcal = 1100 kcal/day. 1100 kcal/day per 9 kcal/g of fat = 122 g/day will be burned.

111. 1100 kcal/day will be burned. Since there are approx. 3500 kcal/lb of body fat, it will take approx. 3 days to lose the 1 lb of body fat.

112. Anorexia nervosa in the severe reduction of food intake so as not to gain weight. Bulimia is recurrent episodes of binge eating along with self-induced vomiting, laxatives, diuretics, strict dieting, fasting, or vigorous exercise to prevent weight gain.

113. a. Radiation: heat is transferred by electromagnetic waves
     b. Conduction: heat moves by direct transfer of thermal energy from molecule to molecule
     c. Convection: warm air or water moves away from the body to be replaced by cooler air
     d. Evaporation: loss of water from the skin and the lining of the respiratory tract carrying body heat with it

114. See Fig. 18-21, page 639.

115. shivering (increased skeletal-muscle activity), shivering thermogenesis

116. vasodilation for heat loss from body to environment, behavioral changes including a change in surface area (curling up in ball to "save" heat or decrease heat loss), change in clothing, change in surroundings

117. water loss from surface of skin and from respiratory lining during expiration (approx. 60 ml/day)

118. On humid days, sweat cannot evaporate. Sweat must evaporate to exert its cooling effects. On nonhumid days, sweat can evaporate and therefore cool.

119. change in skin blood flow

120. sweating and behavioral changes

121. shivering and behavioral changes

122. increase, aldosterone

123. increase in metabolic rate

124. Endogenous pyrogens (interleukin 1, IL-1), tumor necrosis factor (TNF), and inter-leukin 6 (IL-6) are released from monocytes and macrophages during infection or inflammation and have an effect on the temperature-regulating area in the hypo-thalamus.

125. increased heat production from exercising skeletal muscle

CHAPTER
19
REPRODUCTION

Section A. General Terminology and Concepts

1. Diagram the hypothalamic–pituitary–target organ axis for the male and female reproductive system.

GENERAL PRINCIPLES OF GAMETOGENESIS

2. Define gametogenesis.

3. Male gametes are known as _____ , and female gametes are known as _____ .

4. The primary sex hormone in males is _____.

5. The primary sex hormones in females are_____ and _____.

6. The first stage in gametogenesis is _____. The number of chromosomes in each cell is _____.

7. The second stage in gametogenesis is _____.

8. Describe how the first meiotic division differs from the second meiotic division.

9. The number of chromosomes in each gamete following meiosis is _____.

Review the SECTION SUMMARY and REVIEW QUESTIONS at the end of this section in your textbook.

Section B. Male Reproductive Physiology

ANATOMY

10. The primary male reproductive organs are the _____.

11. The accessory male reproductive organs are the _____, _____, and _____.

12. Spermatogenesis occurs in the _____, which are located in the _____.

13. Testosterone is produced by _____ located between the seminiferous tubules.

14. Draw a coronal section of the testes. Label the seminiferous tubules, epididymis, and vas deferens. Indicate where the scrotum is located.

15. Draw anatomically the structures of the male reproductive system. Include the testes, scrotum, epididymis, vas deferens, seminal vesicles, prostate gland, bulbourethral glands, ejaculatory duct, urethra, and penis.

16. Semen is composed of:

SPERMATOGENESIS

17. Draw a sperm. Label the acrosome, head, midpiece, and tail.

18. Describe the function of the acrosome.

19. Genetic information is contained in which part of the sperm?

20. The time for primary spermatocytes to become mature sperm is about _____ days.

21. Spermatogenesis occurs in the _____.

22. Sertoli cells are located in the _____.

23. List the major functions of the Sertoli cells.

   a.

   b.

   c.

   d.

   e.

   f.

   g.

TRANSPORT OF SPERM

24. Describe the pathway of sperm transport starting with the seminiferous tubules.

Erection

25. Erection is a vascular effect brought about by (*parasympathetic, sympathetic*) stimulation and (*parasympathetic, sympathetic*) inhibition of the small arteries of the penis.

26. The inability to achieve or sustain an erection for sexual intercourse is known as _____.

Ejaculation

27. The release of semen from the penis is known as _____.

28. The volume of semen per ejaculate is about _____ ml.

29. The number of sperm per milliliter of ejaculate is about _____.

30. Describe the two phases of ejaculation.

Phase 1:

Phase 2:

31. Erection involves (*stimulation, inhibition*) of sympathetic nerves to the arteries of the penis, and ejaculation involves (*stimulation, inhibition*) of sympathetic nerves to ductal smooth muscle.

HORMONAL CONTROL OF MALE REPRODUCTIVE FUNCTIONS

Control of the Testes

32. Diagram the negative-feedback loop for male reproduction. Include the hypothalamic–anterior–pituitary–target organ axis, GnRH, FSH and LH, testosterone, inhibin, Leydig cells, and Sertoli cells.

33. Bursts of action potentials cause the release of GnRH approximately every ____ h.

34. FSH acts on the _____ cells to aid in _____.

35. LH acts on the _____ cells to stimulate _____ secretion, which aids in spermatogenesis.

36. LH secretion is inhibited by _____ feedback to the _____ or _____.

37. FSH secretion is inhibited by the protein hormone _____ secreted by the _____ cells.

Testosterone

38. Describe the paracrine effect of testosterone on spermatogenesis.

39. Describe the effect of testosterone on the accessory reproductive organs.

40. Describe the effect of testosterone on secondary sex characteristics.

41. Describe the effect of testosterone on growth.

42. Describe the effect of testosterone on behavior.

Mechanism of Action

43. The biologically active form of testosterone in most cells of the body is _____. However, in the brain, testosterone is converted to _____ as the active form of the hormone.

Review the SECTION SUMMARY and REVIEW QUESTIONS at the end of this section in your textbook.

Section C. Female Reproductive Physiology

44. Spermatogenesis is continuous in the male, whereas ovulation is _____ in the female.

45. The length of an average menstrual cycle is about _____ days.

ANATOMY

46. Diagram the female reproductive anatomy. Include the ovaries, uterine tubes, uterus, cervix, and vagina.

OVARIAN FUNCTION

47. Two functions of the ovaries are:

    a.

    b.

Oogenesis

48. Of the 2 to 4 million eggs in the ovaries at birth, about _____ are ovulated during the reproductive lifetime.

49. Oogonia (primitive germ cells) develop into _____ in utero.

50. The germ cells present at birth are _____ with _____ chromosomes, each chromosome containing _____ sister chromatids. These cells are in a state called _____ . The first meiotic division is completed before _____ . The two daughter cells are called _____ and _____ . The second meiotic division is completed after _____, producing one mature ovum and ___ polar bodies.

Follicle Growth

51. Draw an ovarian follicle and label the following: oocyte, granulosa cells, zona pellucida, theca, and antrum.

52. The granulosa cells secrete _____, _____ , and _____.

53. At the beginning of each menstrual cycle, _____ preantral follicles develop into antral follicles. One dominant follicle continues, and the others undergo the process known as _____.

54. The release of secondary oocytes from the follicles onto the surface of the ovary is known as _____, which occurs _____ days before the onset of the next menstrual cycle.

Formation of the Corpus Luteum

55. Describe the corpus luteum.

56. Diagram the two phases of the menstrual cycle and include the major ovarian events in each.

Sites of Secretion of Ovarian Hormones

57.   List the ovarian hormones which are secreted during the two phases of the menstrual cycle. Also indicate the cells from which these hormones are released.

Follicular phase:

Luteal phase:

CONTROL OF OVARIAN FUNCTION

58.   Draw lines representing the FSH, LH, estrogen, and progesterone plasma concentrations during the menstrual cycle. Label the LH surge.

59.   The first rise in plasma estrogen is from estrogen released from the _____.
The second rise in estrogen is from estrogen released from the _____.
The source of the postovulatory rise in progesterone is the _____.

Follicle Development and Estrogen Secretion
During the Early and Middle Follicular Phase

60. FSH stimulates _____ cells to produce estrogen and causes the follicles to grow toward maturity.

61. LH stimulates the theca cells to synthesize _____, which diffuse into the granulosa cells and are converted to _____.

62. Diagram the hormonal feedback loop for ovarian function during the early and middle follicular phases. Include GnRH, FSH, LH, granulosa cells, theca cells, androgens, estrogens, and inhibin.

LH Surge and Ovulation

63. Describe the positive feedback effects of estrogen on LH output.

The Corpus Luteum

64. The major stimulus for the corpus luteum to produce large quantities of estrogen and progesterone is _____.

65. GnRH secretion is (*increased, decreased*) during the luteal phase of the menstrual cycle.

66. Inhibin, secreted by the _____, (*stimulates, inhibits*) FSH secretion.

67. Corpus luteum degeneration after 10 to 14 days may be due to:

68. When the corpus luteum degenerates, will the following hormones increase (I) or decrease (D)?

    a. _____ plasma estrogen

    b. _____ plasma progesterone

    c. _____ GnRH

    d. _____ FSH

    e. _____ LH

UTERINE CHANGES IN THE MENSTRUAL CYCLE

69. The two ovarian phases of the menstrual cycle are:

    a.

    b.

70. The three uterine phases of the menstrual cycle are:

    a.

    b.

    c.

71. Diagram the events that occur during the menstrual cycle. Include ovarian and endometrial events for the corresponding endometrial and ovarian phases.

72. During the proliferative phase, rising estrogen levels have the following effect on the endometrium:

73. During the secretory phase, progesterone is released from the _____ along with _____ .

74. Progesterone has the following effects on the endometrium:

75. Why is it important that progesterone inhibit myometrial contractility during the secretory phase in the uterus?

76. Describe the effects of estrogen and progesterone on cervical mucus.

77. Describe the events that occur when the corpus luteum degenerates.

78. Describe the effects of endometrial prostaglandins.

Review Table 19-2, page 655, and Fig. 19-16, page 667, and Fig. 19-20, page 672.

OTHER EFFECTS OF ESTROGEN AND PROGESTERONE

79. List the major effects of estrogen and progesterone on the body.

80. Describe premenstrual syndrome (PMS).

ANDROGENS IN WOMEN

81. Sources of the low plasma concentrations of androgens in females are:

FEMALE SEXUAL RESPONSE

82. Sex drive in females is primarily dependent on (*androgens, estrogens*).

PREGNANCY

83. After ejaculation, sperm remain fertile for about _____ h.

84. After ovulation, the egg remains fertile for about _____ h.

85. For fertilization to occur, sexual intercourse should occur within _____ h before ovulation to about _____ h after ovulation.

Ovum Transport

86. Once the egg is released from the surface of the ovary (ovulation), it is transported through the _____ to the _____, a process which takes about _____ days.

Sperm Transport and Capacitation

87. The pathway of ejaculated sperm in the female reproductive tract is:

88. Of the several hundred million sperm ejaculated, why do only a few hundred reach the uterine tubes?

89. Capacitation of the sperm involve:

Fertilization

90. Diagram the events that lead to fertilization and the beginning of embryogenesis.

91. If fertilization of the egg does not occur, the egg _____.

92. Tubal and abdominal pregnancies are known as _____ pregnancies.

Early Development, Implantation, and Placentation

93. Define:

    a. Zygote:

    b. Conceptus:

    c. Blastocyst:

    d. Embryo:

    e. Fetus:

94. Implantation is the embedding of the _____ in the endometrium.

95. The source of nutrients for the developing implanted embryo is _____.

96. The structure responsible for nutrient, gas, and waste product exchange after the first 5 weeks of development is the _____.

97. Describe the direction of blood flow for the following:

    a. Uterine artery:

    b. Uterine veins:

    c. Umbilical arteries:

    d. Umbilical vein:

98. Do the fetal and maternal blood "mix" (or come in direct contact with each other) in the placenta?

99. The space formed by the inner cell mass and the trophoblast layer of cells during development is the _____ cavity and is filled with a fluid called _____ fluid.

Hormonal and Other Changes During Pregnancy

100. Diagram the estrogen, progesterone, and chorionic gonadotropin (CG) levels during pregnancy.

101. During the first 2 months of pregnancy the estrogen and progesterone are supplied by the _____ , which is kept "intact" by the action of the hormone _____ released from the _____.

102. Coincidental with the decreased corpus luteum function, large quantities of estrogen and progesterone secretion come from the _____.

103. During pregnancy, GnRH, FSH, and LH levels are (*high, low*). These levels ensure _____ .

Parturition

104. Diagram the factors that stimulate uterine contraction during parturition. Indicate the positive feedback events.

105. Oxytocin is released from the _____. Prostaglandins are released from the _____.

Lactation

106. List the hormones involved in breast development during pregnancy. Indicate their site of origin.

107. Diagram the steps and hormones involved in *milk synthesis*.

108. Diagram the steps and hormones involved in *milk ejection*.

Contraception

109. State the site of action of the following methods of contraception.

   a. Oral contraceptives:

   b. RU486:

   c. IUD:

Review the SUMMARY and REVIEW QUESTIONS at the end of this section in your textbook.

Section D. The Chronology of Reproductive Function

SEX DETERMINATION

110. Sex is determined by the two sex chromosomes. In males, they are _____, and in females, they are _____ .

111. The X chromosome is (*larger, smaller*) than the Y chromosome.

SEX DIFFERENTIATION

Differentiation of the Gonads

112. Testes begin to develop if the _____ gene is present on the ___ chromosome. In the absence of the _____ chromosome, ovaries develop.

Differentiation of Internal and External Genitalia

113. Diagram the steps and hormones involves in male differentiation of internal and external genitalia.

114. Diagram the steps and hormones involved in female differentiation of internal and external genitalia.

PUBERTY

115. Puberty normally occurs between the ages of _____.

116. The onset of puberty may be caused by:

117. Menarche is:

MENOPAUSE

118. The cessation of menstrual cycles is known as _____. This usually occurs at about _____ years of age.

119. The time period of menstrual irregularity ending with menopause is known as _____.

120. Following menopause, circulating levels of estrogens are (*elevated, normal, low*).

Review the SUMMARY and REVIEW QUESTIONS at the end of this section and the THOUGHT QUESTIONS at the end of this chapter in your textbook.

CHAPTER 19 ANSWER KEY

1. See Fig. 19-1, page 649.

2. Gametogenesis is the production of reproductive cells (gametes).

3. sperm, ova

4. testosterone

5. estrogen, progesterone

6. mitosis, 46

7. meiosis

8. See Fig. 19-2, page 650, and Fig. 19-6, page 654.

9. 23

10. testes

11. ducts, glands, and penis

12. seminiferous tubules, testes

13. Interstitial cells of Leydig

14. See Fig. 19-4, page 652.

15. See Fig. 19-5, page 653.

16. sperm and secretions from the prostate gland, seminal vesicles, and bulbourethral glands

17. See Fig. 19-7, page 655.

18. The acrosome contains enzymes that are important in the sperms' penetration of the ovum.

19. the nucleus which is in the head of the sperm

20. 64

21. seminiferous tubules

22. seminiferous tubules

23. a. provide blood-testis barrier to chemicals
    b. nourish developing sperm
    c. secrete luminal fluid, including androgen-binding protein
    d. receive stimulation by testosterone and FSH to secrete paracrine agents that stimulate sperm production and maturation
    e. secrete the protein hormone inhibin, which inhibits FSH secretion
    f. phagocytize defective sperm
    g. secrete, during embryonic life, Müllerian inhibiting factor, which causes the primordial female duct system to regress

24. seminiferous tubules to rete testes to efferent ductules to epididymis to vas deferens to ejaculatory duct to urethra

25. parasympathetic, sympathetic

26. impotence

27. ejaculation

28. 3

29. 100 million/ml

30. Phase 1: Emission—sympathetic stimulation causes the smooth muscle of the epididymis, vas deferens, ejaculatory ducts, and seminal vesicles to contract, thus emptying the sperm and secretion into the urethra.
    Phase 2: The urethral smooth muscle contraction expels semen from the urethra.

31. inhibition, stimulation

32. See Fig. 19-10, page 658.

33. 2

34. Sertoli, spermatogenesis

35. Leydig, testosterone

36. testosterone, hypothalamus, anterior pituitary

37. inhibin, Sertoli

38. Testosterone from the Leydig cells enters the Sertoli cells and, via these cells, facilitates spermatogenesis.

39. Testosterone induces differentiation of the male duct system, glands, and penis and maintains their functions (secretion, erection, ejaculation).

40. Testosterone causes beard growth, characteristic hair distribution, deepening of the voice, and the masculine pattern of fat distribution.

41. Testosterone stimulates bone growth indirectly by stimulating GH secretion and shuts off bone growth by causing closure of epiphyseal plates. Anabolic steroids increase the muscle mass.

42. Testosterone develops the sex drive at puberty and maintains the sex drive in adult males.

43. dihydrotestosterone, estradiol

44. cyclic

45. 28

46. See Fig. 19-11, page 662.

47. a. oogenesis
    b. secretion of estrogens, progesterones, and inhibin

48. 400

49. primary oocytes

50. primary oocytes, 46, 2, meiotic arrest, ovulation, secondary oocyte, first polar body, fertilization, three

51. See Fig. 19-14, page 665.

52. estrogen, progesterone, inhibin

53. 10 to 25, atresia

54. ovulation, 14

55. The corpus luteum is the structure left behind on the surface of the ovary after ovulation, which secretes, estrogen, progesterone, and inhibin. If fertilization does not occur, it lasts about 10 days and then degenerates.

56. See Fig. 19-15, page 666.

57. Follicular phase: estrogen, progesterone, and inhibin from granulosa cells (progesterone also from thecal cells)
    Luteal phase: estrogen, progesterone, and inhibin from corpus luteum

58. See Fig. 19-16, page 667.

59. ovarian follicle, corpus luteum, corpus luteum

60. granulosa

61. androgens, estrogens

62. See Fig. 19-18, page 669.

63. As the estrogen level rises rapidly during the late follicular phase, it exerts a positive feedback to increase LH output, which will cause ovulation.

64. LH

65. decreased

66. corpus luteum, inhibits

67. production of a paracrine, maybe prostaglandins, which interferes with the corpus luteum's activities

68. a. D   c. I   e. I
    b. D   d. I

69. a. follicular   b. luteal

70. a. menstrual   b. proliferative   c. secretory

71. See Fig. 19-20, page 672.

72. increase the thickness of the endometrium and induce progesterone receptors in the endometrium

73. corpus luteum, estrogen

74. increases secretory activity in the endometrium, increases vascularity, increases glycogen, increases glandularity, and inhibits myometrial contractions

75. Progesterone prevents the fertilized egg from being removed after implantation in the uterus.

76. Estrogen: mucus is clear, nonviscous, and abundant to allow sperm to move easily through the uterus toward the uterine tubes where fertilization normally occurs. Progesterone: mucus becomes thick and sticky, acting as a plug to prevent bacteria from entering the uterus (and possibly affecting the fetus).

77. Plasma estrogen and progesterone levels fall, which leads to contraction of the uterus due to constriction of the uterine blood vessels. Thus the endometrial lining sloughs off (menses).

78. Endometrial prostaglandins mediate vasoconstriction and uterine smooth-muscle contraction. They also affect smooth-muscle elsewhere in the body and may cause the symptoms of nausea, vomiting, headaches, and cramps.

79. See Table 19-8, page 674.

80. PMS is a cluster of distressing physical and psychological symptoms occurring just before menstruation and relieved shortly after the onset of menstruation. Symptoms

may include several of the following: painful breasts, bloating, headache, backache, depression, anxiety, irritability, as well as other behavioral and motor changes.

81. ovaries and adrenal cortex

82. androgens

83. 48

84. 10 to 15

85. 48, 15

86. uterine tubes, uterus, four

87. vagina to uterus to uterine tubes

88. The acid environment in the vagina causes mortality. The distance traveled and energy required also cause significant sperm mortality.

89. changes in the sperm tail and sperm membrane

90. See Fig. 19–21, page 676.

91. disintegrates

92. ectopic

93. a. fertilized egg
    b. fertilized egg and all its derivatives throughout pregnancy
    c. stage of cell division consisting of the trophoblast (an inner cell mass) and a central fluid-filled cavity
    d. developing human being during the first 2 months of intrauterine development
    e. developing human being after the first 2 months of intrauterine development

94. blastocyst

95. endometrial lining

96. placenta

97. a. blood flow from mother to placenta
    b. blood flow from placenta to mother
    c. blood flow from fetus to placenta
    d. blood flow from placenta to fetus

98. no

99. amniotic, amniotic

100. See Fig. 19–26, page 681.

101. corpus luteum, HCG, trophoblastic cells of the developing embryo

102. placenta

103. low, no folicular development or ovulation during pregnancy

104. See Fig. 19-28, page 685.

105. anterior pituitary, uterus

106. estrogen from the placenta, progesterone from the placenta, prolactin from the anterior pituitary, placental lactogen from the placenta

107. See Fig. 19-30, page 687.

108. See Fig. 19-30, page 687.

109. a. (combination of estrogen and progesterone) inhibit interior pituitary gonado-trophin release and therefore prevent ovulation. The progestin component inhibits endometrial proliferation and therefore makes implantation difficult.
    b. binds competitively to the progesterone receptors but does not activate them
    c. interferes with implantation in the uterus

110. X and Y, X and X

111. larger

112. SRY, Y, Y

113. See Fig. 19-31A, page 694.

114. See Fig. 19-31B, page 694.

115. 10 and 14

116. changes in brain function responsible for the release of GnRH

117. the onset of the first menstrual period, usually about 12 years of age

118. menopause, 50

119. climacteric

120. low

CHAPTER
20
DEFENSE MECHANISMS OF THE BODY

Section A. Immunology: Defenses Against Foreign Matter

1. The two categories of immune defenses are:

   a.

   b.

2. Differentiate between bacteria and viruses.

CELLS MEDIATING IMMUNE DEFENSES

3. Describe the origin and functions of the following cells:

   a. Plasma cells:

   b. Macrophages:

   c. Mast cells:

NONSPECIFIC IMMUNE DEFENSES

4. Nonspecific immune defenses include:

    a.

    b.

    c.

Defenses at Body Surfaces

5. List specialized defenses at the body surfaces that aid in immunity.

Inflammation

6. The major function of inflammation is:

7. The general cell type involved in inflammation is the _____; specific cells of this type include _____, _____ , and _____ .

8. The five phases of inflammation are:

    a.

    b.

    c.

    d.

    e.

9. What are the adaptive values of each of the above.

    a.

    b.

    c.

    d.

    e.

10. Describe the membrane attack complex (MAC).

11. List some other functions of complement proteins.

Interferon

12. Interferon nonspecifically interferes with _____ replication inside host cells.

13. Explain by means of a diagram how interferon interferes with this replication.

SPECIFIC IMMUNE DEFENSES

Overview

14. The cells that mediate specific immune responses are _____.

15. A foreign molecule that triggers a specific immune response is called a(n) _____.

16. The three stages of a specific immune response are:

    a.

    b.

    c.

17. Discuss the important aspects of each of the above stages of the specific immune response.

    a.

    b.

    c.

Lymphoid Organs and Lymphocyte Types

Lymphoid organs

18. Primary lymphoid organs include:

19. Peripheral lymphoid organs include:

20. Specific immune responses occur in (*primary, peripheral*) lymphoid organs.

Lymphocyte origins

21. The type of lymphocyte that matures in bone marrow is the (*B, T*) lymphocyte, and the type that matures in the thymus is the (*B, T*) lymphocyte. These cells move on to the (*primary, peripheral*) lymphoid organs where mitosis produces identical offspring. A third lymphocyte that does not manifest specific immunity for antigens is the _____.

Functions of B Cells and T Cells

22. Diagram the roles and interactions of the B, cytotoxic T, and helper T cells.

23. Protein chemical messengers that regulate immune responses and are secreted by lymphocytes, monocytes, and macrophages are called _____.

24. Their functions include:

25. List some important cytokines.

Lymphocyte Receptors

26. B-cell receptors are _____, which can be divided into the following five classes:

27. Diagram a B-cell receptor (antibody). Indicate the Fc portion and the antigen binding site.

28. T cells can bind with antigen only when the antigen complexes with the cell's _____ proteins. Cells with these complexes are called _____.

29. The two classes of MHC proteins are:

    a.

    b.

30. Cytotoxic and suppressor T cells require _____ proteins. Helper T cells require _____ proteins.

Antigen Presentation to T Cells

Presentation to helper T cells

31. Describe by means of a diagram how macrophages present antigen to helper T cells.

32. Describe by means of a diagram how B cells present antigen to helper T cells.

NK Cells

33. Differentiate between cytotoxic T cells and NK cells.

Antibody-Mediated Immune Responses: Defenses Against Bacteria, Extracellular Viruses, and Toxins

34. Describe by means of a diagram the role of the helper T cells and cytokines in B-cell activation.

35. Indicate the correct class of antibody, i.e., IgG, IgM, IgE, IgA, or IgD.

    a. _____ most abundant class of antibodies

    b. _____ provide specific immunity against bacteria and viruses

    c. _____ mediate allergic responses

    d. _____ act at site of body linings and body surfaces

36. How do the antibodies bound to antigens actually "kill" the microbe or foreign substance involved?

37. Differentiate between active and passive immunity.

38. Describe by means of a diagram the role of cytotoxic T cells in destroying virus-infected or cancer cells.

39. Describe by means of a diagram the role of NK cells and activated macrophages in destroying virus-infected or cancer cells.

40. List several cytokines secreted by helper T cells.

41. Describe how immunotherapy can be used to destroy cancer cells.

SYSTEMIC MANIFESTATIONS OF INFECTION

42. List the acute phase (adaptive) responses to infection.

FACTORS THAT ALTER THE BODY'S RESISTANCE TO INFECTION

43. List some major factors that alter the body's resistance to infection.

44. AIDS is caused by _____ containing (*RNA, DNA*).

45. The cells primarily affected by the AIDS virus are _____.

46. The time from HIV infection to full-blown AIDS is normally about _____ years.

47. The transmission routes for HIV are:

48. The primary drug of choice for the treatment of AIDS is _____. Its mechanism of action is:

HARMFUL IMMUNE RESPONSES

Graft Rejection

49. List some immune responses that can be *harmful* to the body.

50. How does cyclosporin aid in preventing graft rejection?

Transfusion Reactions

51. An AB$^+$ individual has the following blood antigens and antibodies with respect to the ABO and Rh factors:

52. O$^+$ blood (packed cells) can be transfused safely into individuals with the following blood types:

53. O$^-$ blood (packed cells) can be transfused safely into individuals with the following blood types:

54. An Rh$^-$ mother carrying an Rh$^+$ fetus may develop _____ at the time of delivery. In future pregnancies, fetal erythrocyte destruction may occur—a condition known as _____.
    In order to prevent this condition, the following may be done:

Allergy (Hypersensitivity)

55. Differentiate among delayed hypersensitivity, immune complex hypersensitivity, and immediate hypersensitivity.

Autoimmune Disease

56. List three autoimmune diseases and what part of the body is being "attacked" for each disease.

Review Table 20-12, page 734.

Review the SUMMARY and REVIEW QUESTIONS at the end of this section in your textbook.

Section B. Nonimmune Metabolism of Foreign Chemicals

57. By means of a diagram, explain how the body defends against nonmicrobial foreign chemicals.

58. The main site of foreign chemical biotransformation is in the _____, where the microsomal enzyme system (MES) transforms chemicals into (*more polar, less soluble, less polar, more soluble*) substances. Thus the foreign chemical's tubular reabsorption is (*enhanced, diminished*) and urinary excretion is (*facilitated, inhibited*).

Review the SUMMARY and REVIEW QUESTIONS at the end of this section in your textbook.

Section C. Hemostasis: The Prevention of Blood Loss

59. Define:

    a. Hemostasis:

    b. Hematoma:

FORMATION OF A PLATELET PLUG

60. The plasma protein secreted by endothelial cells and platelets that forms a bridge between the endothelial vessel wall and platelets is _____.

61. Platelet aggregation which leads to a platelet plug is enhanced when platelets release chemical agents from their secretory vesicles such as _____ and synthesize substances such as _____.

62. Platelets are able to contract and seal small breaks in blood vessel walls because platelets contain a very high concentration of _____.

63. Platelet plugs do not continuously expand from the damaged site into the normal endothelium because normal endothelial cells release _____, which are inhibitors of platelet aggregation.

BLOOD COAGULATION: CLOT FORMATION

64. Differentiate between the intrinsic and extrinsic pathways for blood clotting.

65. Diagram the external pathway for clot formation.

66. The "final" plasma protein in the clotting process that "traps" erythrocytes is _____.

67. Describe the two major roles the liver plays in the clotting process.

    a.

    b.

ANTICLOTTING SYSTEMS

Factors That Oppose Clot Formation

68. Three naturally occurring anticoagulants or factors that limit the clotting system are:

The Fibrinolytic System

69. The fibrinolytic system *dissolves* a clot by activating plasminogen to _____, which digests _____, thereby dissolving the clot.

70. Tissue plasminogen activator (t-PA) is secreted by _____ and is activated by _____.

ANTICLOTTING DRUGS

71. List several anticlotting drugs and explain the mechanism of action of each.

Review the SUMMARY and REVIEW QUESTIONS at the end of this section in your textbook.

Section D. Resistance to Stress

FUNCTIONS OF CORTISOL IN STRESS

72. List some major functions of increased cortisol during stress.

FUNCTIONS OF THE SYMPATHETIC NERVOUS SYSTEM IN STRESS

73. List some major functions of the sympathetic nervous system and epinephrine during stress.

OTHER HORMONES RELEASED DURING STRESS

74. List other hormones often involved in the stress response. [Indicate whether these hormones are increased (I) or decreased (D) during stress.]

Review the SUMMARY and REVIEW QUESTIONS at the end of this section and the THOUGHT QUESTIONS at the end of this chapter in your textbook.

CHAPTER 20 ANSWER KEY

1. a. nonspecific immunity   b. specific immunity

2. Bacteria are unicellular organisms (prokaryocytes) with a cell wall and plasma membrane and no intracellular membrane-bound organelles. Viruses are nucleic acids surrounded by a protein coat. They cannot replicate by themselves and must "live" inside other cells.

3. a. differentiate from B lymphocytes, are found in tissues, synthesize and secrete antibodies
   b. derived from monocytes, are found in many organs, and tissues of the body, engulf microbes and other foreign particles
   c. differentiate from bone marrow cells, found in many organs and tissues, secrete various chemical messengers

4. a. defenses at body surfaces   b. inflammation   c. interferons

5. an intact skin, mucus secretion from respiratory and upper gastrointestinal tracts which contain antimicrobial agents, hairs in the nose, cough and sneeze reflexes, acid secretion from the stomach, surface (skin) microbes

6. to destroy or inactivate foreign material and set the stage for tissue repair

7. phagocyte, neutrophils, macrophages, monocytes

8. a. vasodilation and increased permeability to proteins
   b. chemotaxis
   c. killing by phagocytes
   d. complement
   e. tissue repair

9. a. Vasodilation increases blood flow to inflamed areas, leading to increased delivery of leukocytes.
   b. Chemotaxins (chemical mediators) attract phagocytes to the area of inflammation that has the invading microbes.
   c. Opsonins (chemical substances produced by the body) help bind the phagocytes to the microbes and therefore enhance phagocytosis.
   d. Complement are plasma proteins that become activated through a cascade system and inactivate microbes without phagocytosis.
   e. Fibroblasts rapidly divide and secrete large quantities of collagen for repair of damaged areas.

10. Five of the proteins generated in the complement cascade form a complex that becomes embedded in the microbial plasma membrane and causes microbial membrane channels to become leaky to salt and water, thus lysing the cells.

11. direct destruction of invading cells by membrane attack complex (MAC), vasodilation and increased capillary permeability to proteins, chemotaxis, enhancement of phagocytosis (opsonization)

12. viral

13. See Fig. 20-5, page 707.

14. lymphocytes

15. antigen

16. a. antigen encounter and recognition by lymphocytes
    b. lymphocyte activation
    c. the attack

17. a. Lymphocytes have specific plasma membrane receptors that recognize "specific" antigens.
    b. Antigen binding to the lymphocyte receptors activates the lymphocytes to undergo mitotic division. These cells then differentiate into specific cell types.
    c. Activated and differentiated lymphocytes attack the antigens that initiated the response. B cells secrete antibodies, and cytotoxic T cells kill the antigen-bearing cells.

18. bone marrow and thymus

19. lymph nodes, spleen, tonsils, and lymphocyte accumulations in the linings of the intestinal, respiratory, genital, and urinary tracts

20. peripheral

21. B, T, peripheral, NK (natural killer) cell

22. See Fig. 20-7, page 711.

23. cytokines

24. local effects on immune cells, hormone-like effects on host defense organs and tissues, inflammatory mediators

25. 12 interleukins, 4 colony-stimulating factors, 3 interferons, 2 tumor necrosis factors

26. immunoglobulins; IgA, IgD, IgE, IgG, IgM

27. See Fig. 20-8, page 712.

28. MHC, antigen-presenting cells (APCs)

29. a. class I: on surfaces of all nucleated cells
    b. class II: on surfaces of macrophages and B cells

30. class I, class II

31. See Fig. 20-9A, page 714.

32. See Fig. 20-9B, page 714.

33. NK cells are not antigen-specific, whereas T and B cells have specific receptors on their surfaces. NK cells can attack virus-infected cells or cancer cells without any specific recognition by the NK cell.

34. See Fig. 20-11, page 718.

35. a. IgG
    b. IgG and IgM
    c. IgE
    d. IgA

36. The antibody-antigen complex activates complement, macrophages, or NK cells which will "kill" the microbe or foreign substance. Figures 20-12 and 20-13.

37. Active immunity involves antibody formation in response to the foreign antigen. The initial response is slow and requires several days (primary response). Subsequent exposure to the same foreign antigen results in an immediate and increased antibody production mediated by memory B cells (secondary response). Passive immunity is the direct transfer of actively formed antibodies from one individual to the next.

38. See Fig. 20-15, page 722.

39. See Fig. 20-16, page 723.

40. interleukin-2, interleukin-6, gamma interferon

41. Treat tumor-specific cytotoxic T cells from the person's tumor with IL-2, to cause cell proliferation and enhanced tumoricidal ability, and then inject these cells back into the individual to kill the tumor cells.

42. fever, a decrease in plasma concentrations of iron and zinc, secretion by the liver of acute-phase proteins, release of neutrophils and monocytes by bone marrow, release of amino acids from muscle

43. protein-calorie malnutrition, preexisting infection, stress, psychological state, a genetic deficiency of antibody synthesis (immunodeficiency)

44. retrovirus, RNA

45. helper T cells

46. 5 to 10

47. contaminated blood products; sexual intercourse with an infected partner; infected mother to offspring during pregnancy, delivery, or breastfeeding

48. zidovudine (AZT). It blocks the action of the enzyme that converts the viral RNA into the host cell DNA.

49. graft rejection, transfusion reactions, allergies, autoimmune responses, excessive inflammatory reactions to microbes

50. Cyclosporin blocks the production of IL-2 and other cytokines by helper T cells, which decreases proliferation of the cytotoxic T cells.

51. A antigens and B antigens, Rh antigens, no antibodies to these antigens

52. A^+, B^+, AB^+, O^+

53. A^+, A^-, B^+, B^-, AB^+, AB^-, O^+, O^-

54. anti-Rh antibodies, hemolytic disease of the newborn (erythroblastosis fetalis), give Rh^- mother delivering an Rh^+ baby human gammaglobulin against Rh^+ erythrocytes within 72 h after delivery of the Rh^+ baby

55. Delayed hypersensitivity is due to helper T-cell cytokines and microphages; it is slow to develop (several days) and is independent of antibodies. Immune complex hypersensitivity occurs when antibodies complex with antigens, which activates complement, which then induces an inflammatory response. Immediate hypersensitivity occurs when antigens bind to IgE antibodies, which are bound to mast cells. The mast cells then release inflammatory mediators (such as histamines).

56. myasthenia gravis: attacks skeletal-muscle ACh receptors; rheumatoid arthritis: attacks joints; insulin-dependent diabetes mellitus: attacks the beta cells of the pancreas

57. See Fig. 20-19, page 739.

58. liver; more polar, less soluble; diminished; facilitated

59. a. elimination of bleeding   b. accumulation of blood in the tissues

60. von Willebrand factor (VWF)

61. ADP and serotonin, thromboxane A_2

62. actin and myosin

63. PGI_2 and nitric oxide (NO)

64. intrinsic pathway: everything necessary for blood clotting is present in the blood; extrinsic pathway: a cellular element outside the blood is needed.

65. See Fig. 20-24, page 745.

66. fibrin

67. a. The liver produces many of the clotting factors.
    b. Bile salts from the liver are necessary for absorption of vitamin K, which the liver needs to produce prothrombin and other clotting factors.

68. tissue factor pathway inhibitor (TFPI), thrombin's activation of protein C, antithrombin III

69. plasmin, fibrin

70. endothelial cells, fibrin in a clot

71. aspirin: inhibits the cyclooxygenase system that generates thromboxane A_2 which is important in platelet aggregation; oral anticoagulants: interfere with the action of vitamin K; heparin: interferes with platelet function

72. The increased cortisol "mobilizes" fuels (increases plasma concentrations of amino acids, glucose, glycerol, and free fatty acids), increases vascular responsiveness to stimuli such as norepinephrine, and provides anti-inflammatory effects.

73. Increased liver and muscle glycogenolysis, increased breakdown of fat triacylglycerols, decreased fatigue of skeletal muscle, increased cardiac output secondary to increased heart rate and contractility, shunting of blood from viscera to exercising skeletal muscle, increased ventilation, increased blood coagulability

74. Aldosterone (I), vasopressin (ADH) (I), growth hormone (I), glucagon (I), prolactin (I), thyroid hormone, (I), pituitary gonadotrophins (D), sex steroids (D), insulin (D)